Landscapes of CYPRUS

a countryside guide

Third edition

Geoff Daniel

SUNFLOWER
BOOKS

For Richard and Charlotte

Updated printing 2000
Third edition 1998

ISBN 1-85691-106-3

In the Troodos Mountain

Important note to the reader

We have tried to ensure that the descriptions and maps in this book ar error-free at press date. **This printing was updated in August 2000 (se 'Stop Press', beginning on page 124)**. Travellers to Cyprus will be awar of recent changes in the naming of major towns and cities, such a Lefkosia for Nicosia, and Lemesos for Limassol. This is part of officia moves to create a stronger national identity in the Greek part of th island. We have indicated the major changes, but you may encounte others. It will be very helpful for us to receive your comments (sent i care of the publishers, please) for the updating of future printings.

We also rely on those who use this book — especially walkers — t take along a good supply of common sense when they explore. Condi tions change fairly rapidly on Cyprus, and ***storm damage or bulldozin may make a route unsafe at any time***. If the route is not as we outlin it here, and your way ahead is not secure, return to the point c departure. ***Never attempt to complete a tour or walk under hazardou conditions!*** Please read carefully the notes on pages 19 and 39 to 47 as well as the introductory comments at the beginning of each tour an walk (regarding road conditions, equipment, grade, distances and time etc). Explore ***safely***, while at the same time respecting the beauty of th countryside.

Cover photograph: Ayii Saranta (Walk 28)
Title page: Mt Adelphi signpost

Photographs: the author
Maps: John Theasby and Pat Underwood
Plans: John Underwood
Drawings: Katharina Kelly
A CIP catalogue record for this book is available from the British Library
Printed and bound in the UK by Brightsea Press, Exeter

10 9 8 7 6 5 4

Contents

Preface

Cyprus, birthplace of the mythical love goddess Aphrodite, yields its greatest pleasures to the visitor who makes an effort towards closer acquaintance.

If you are content with sun, sand, surf and soured brandy, then you won't be disappointed. But deeper exploration of this special island, on foot or on wheels, coupled with a healthy curiosity about its people and its traditions, will reward you with experiences to treasure a lifetime. Should your first visit to Cyprus be the start of an incurable love affair, do not be at all surprised!

This Third edition of *Landscapes of Cyprus* is divided into three main sections, each with its own introduction.

For **motorists**, there are up-to-date car tours, taking in lively resorts, picturesque villages, mountain spectacle, fast new roads and very slow old ones. There are suggestions for 4WD enthusiasts too.

Picnickers can take their choice of authorised sites with benches and barbecue facilities, or out-of-the-way locations along the course of a walk.

Walkers have a comprehensive guide to Cyprus on foot, totally revised and updated. The walks cover most areas of the island, most are within the stride of anyone sound in wind and limb, and they are easily accessible.

Cyprus — past

The turbulent history of Cyprus dates back to the Stone Age, and the island has undergone numerous changes of 'ownership' over the centuries. Turks, Romans, Greeks, Venetians, and the British have all played a part in the island's destiny. In Nicosia the Cyprus Museum and the Museum of National Struggle are well worth visiting to gain an appreciation of the past.

Throughout the island, richly historic sites beckon the curious traveller, not least the imposing 13th-century castle at Kolossi, Nicosia's Venetian walls, the ancient Tombs of the Kings at Paphos, and the Neolithic settlement at Khirokitia.

In the mountainous Troodos region, nine churches on UNESCO's World Heritage list are rightly famous for beautiful frescoes painted between the 11th and 15th centuries.

Cyprus — present

Since 1960, Cyprus has been an independent republic within the British Commonwealth. In 1974 Turkey occupied the north and northeastern regions, physically dividing the island and establishing a state which remains unrecognised in the international community. It is now possible to travel freely between the two sectors except for a 24-hour period (through the Ledra checkpoint in Nicosia). *Landscapes of Cyprus* therefore regrettably confines its coverage to the south. A future edition might incorporate the Turkish-controlled area, if the political situation changes.

Cyprus — people

For all their recent upheavals, Greek Cypriots remain among the most cheerful, gregarious and hospitable folk you could ever meet. English is taught in schools and widely understood, but even a stumbling attempt at a few words of Greek (see page 45) on the part of the visitor is warmly appreciated. Cypriot hospitality is legendary — *kopiaste!* — and should always be accepted, even i sparingly.

Cyprus — environment

Walking, and other leisure activities which respect the island's sometime fragile environment, will become increasingly important as conventional coast-based tourism heads towards saturation point. The creation of a national park in the beautiful Akamas region in the west is a positive move to ensure protection of sensitive areas such as the green turtle nesting grounds at Lara Beach.

Acknowledgements

I am indebted to the following:

For maps and plans: the Department of Lands and Surveys, Nicosia.

For support and practical assistance: Lillian Panayi, Tourism Officer o the Cyprus Tourism Organisation, London; Noel Josephides (London and Lucy Zenonos (Paphos) of Sunvil Travel; David Pearlman and Ja Horton of ExAlt Travel, Paphos; Yiannis Christofides, the Hote Minerva, Platres; Adrian Akers-Douglas of the Laona Project, Limassol

For new walks: Jan Horton (10) and Adrian Akers-Douglas (12, 21, 22)

Books

It must be emphasised that *Landscapes of Cyprus* is a guide to countryside exploration and intended to be used in addition to a standard guide such as the *Blue Guide Cyprus* (A & C Black). Christos Georgiades *Nature of Cyprus — environment, flora and fauna,* available on the island, is a valuable pictorial reference work; Colin Thubron's *Journe into Cyprus,* an account of a pre-1974 walk round the island, is a scholarly but absorbing read; and Lawrence Durrell's classic, *Bitte Lemons,* is an amusing and poignant portrait of a Cyprus long gone.

Getting about

A **hired car** is undoubtedly the most practical way of exploring Cyprus. Numerous companies offer a wide range of vehicles, from runabouts to prestige models. Small 4WD soft-tops are increasingly popular, and their modest extra cost is worth considering if you plan trips into mountains or remote regions — such is the rough condition of many minor road surfaces. I have included some 4WD route suggestions in this new edition.

Coach tours operate from the main tourist centres, and offer a painless introduction to road conditions and a comfortable view of island scenery.

Inter-town buses are an inexpensive way of moving from one place to another, perhaps for tackling a walk out of a different centre from your hotel base.

Taxis operate in profusion in the towns, more sparsely in villages, and all are identified by a prefix 'T' to the registration number. Rates are fixed by the authorities, and urban taxis are obliged to operate a meter on all journeys. Fares are not high, but on longer journeys it is wise to agree a price in advance. In town you will likely ride in a new Mercedes, but in a village it will probably be something older and more interesting!

Service taxis are a useful way of getting from town to town if you're not in a hurry. They ply between major centres approximately every half-hour and will pick you up at your hotel and take you anywhere central at your destination, picking up and dropping off other passengers en route. They are useful on walks which end on a service taxi route: simply ask a bar or café owner to request a service taxi stop on its next run. Rates are very cheap for the service offered. You will share your journey with other passengers (possibly in a minibus), but this is the only inconvenience.

Local buses are not very helpful for the walker; essentially they bring village folk to town in early morning and take them home later in the day. I would urge you to collect an up-to-date timetable (including fare details) and taxi operator list from any tourist office as soon as you arrive on Cyprus, and to check the availability of any extra seasonal services. Bus, taxi and service taxi departure points in major centres are shown on pages 8 to 13.

NICOSIA (LEFKOSIA)

1 Arts and crafts centre
2 Tourist information
3 Post office
4 Municipal library
5 Town hall
6 Museum of the National Struggle
7 Folk art museum
8 Archbishop's palace and Makarios Cultural Centre
9 Municipal cultural centre
10 Police station
11 Cyprus Museum
12 Telephone, telegraph
13 Municipal theatre
14 House of Representatives
15 Hospital
16 UK high commission
17 Cyprus Airways
18 US embassy
19 Museum (contemporary art)
20 Stadium
21 German embassy
🚗1 Acropolis, Makris, Kypros
🚗2 Kyriakos
🚗3 Karydas
🚌1 Lefkaritis Bus Co
🚌2 Kemek Bus Co
🚌3 Clarios Bus Co
🚌4 EMAN Bus Co

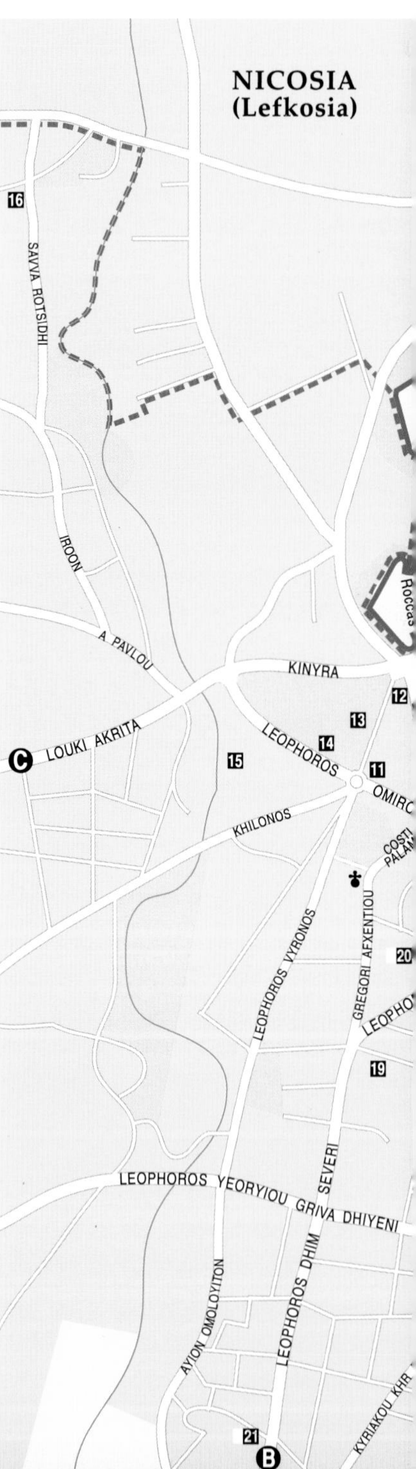

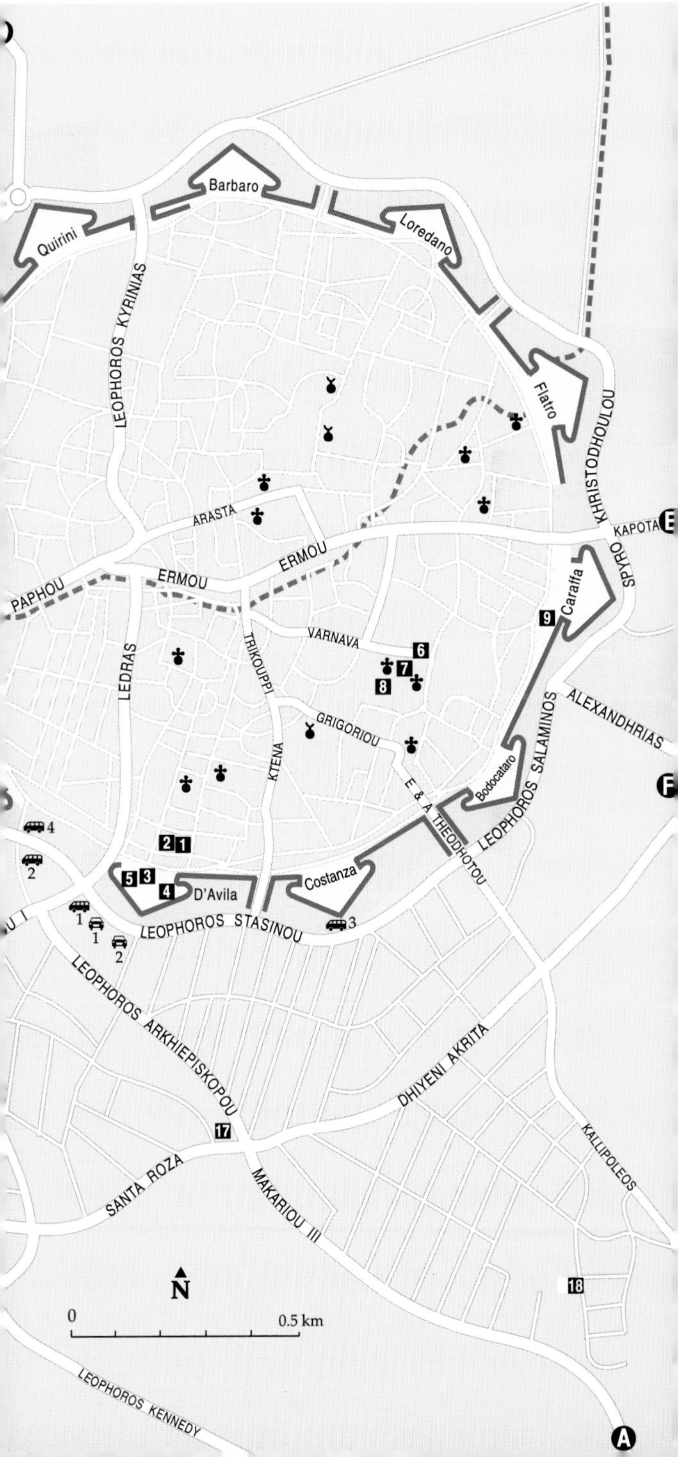

Barbaro
Quirini
Loredano
Flatro
Caraffa
Bodocataro
Costanza
D'Avila
LEOPHOROS KYRINIAS
KHRISTODHOULOU
KAPOTA
SPYRO
ARASTA
ERMOU
ERMOU
PAPHOU
LEDRAS
TRIKOUPPI
KTENA
VARNAVA
GRIGORIOU
E & A THEODHOTOU
LEOPHOROS SALAMINOS
ALEXANDHRIAS
LEOPHOROS STASINOU
LEOPHOROS ARKHIEPISKOPOU
MAKARIOU III
DHIYENI AKRITA
SANTA ROZA
KALLIPOLEOS
LEOPHOROS KENNEDY
N
0
0.5 km

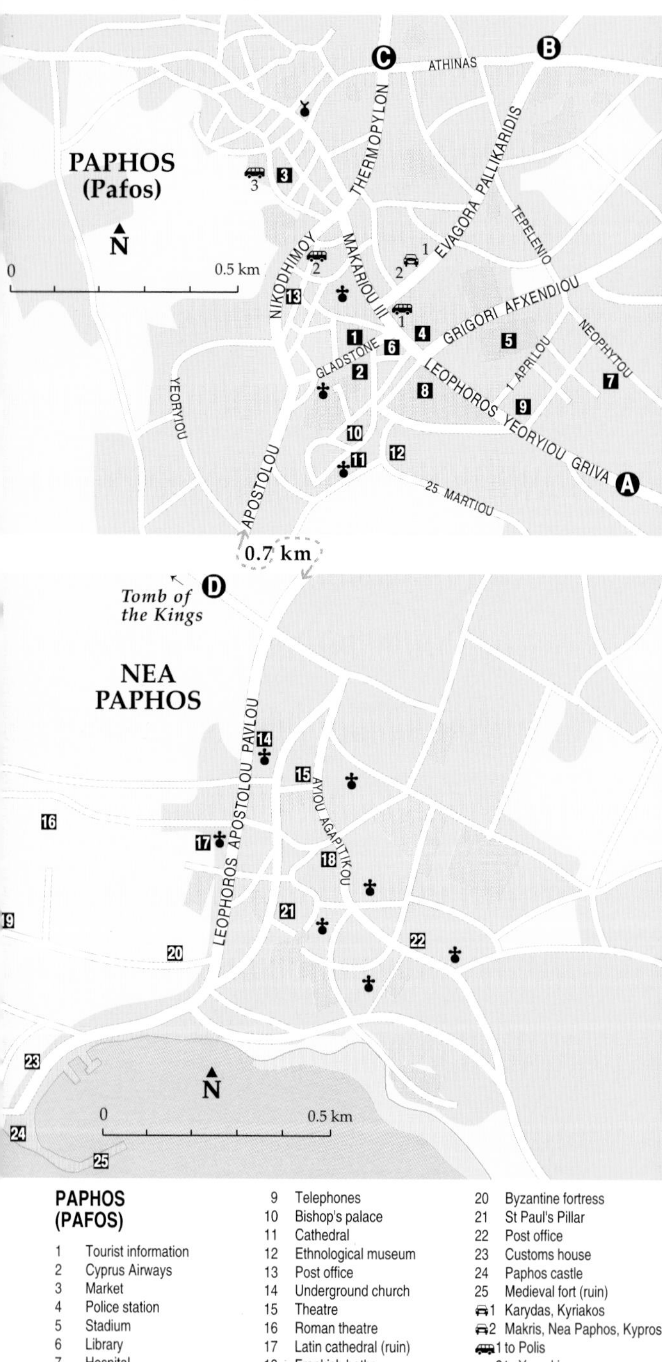

PAPHOS (PAFOS)

1 Tourist information
2 Cyprus Airways
3 Market
4 Police station
5 Stadium
6 Library
7 Hospital
8 Town hall
9 Telephones
10 Bishop's palace
11 Cathedral
12 Ethnological museum
13 Post office
14 Underground church
15 Theatre
16 Roman theatre
17 Latin cathedral (ruin)
18 Frankish baths
19 House of Dionysos
20 Byzantine fortress
21 St Paul's Pillar
22 Post office
23 Customs house
24 Paphos castle
25 Medieval fort (ruin)
🚗1 Karydas, Kyriakos
🚗2 Makris, Nea Paphos, Kypros
🚌1 to Polis
🚌2 to Yeroskipos
🚌3 to Limassol

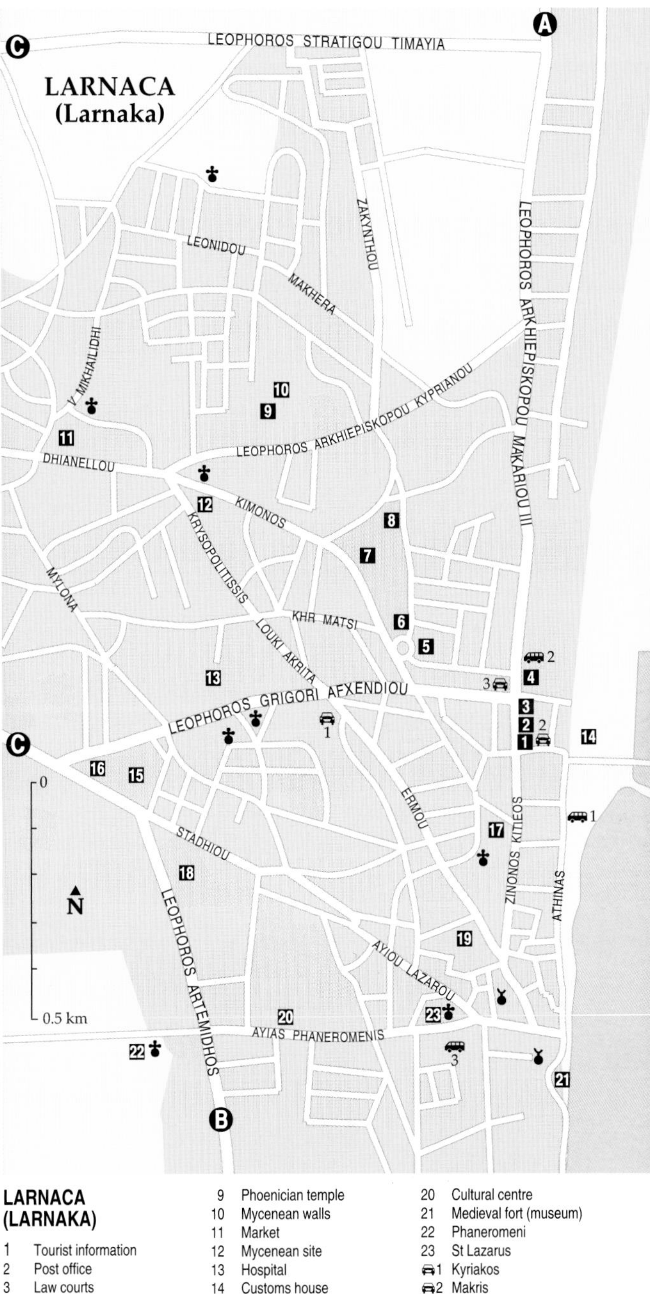

LARNACA (LARNAKA)

1 Tourist information
2 Post office
3 Law courts
4 Police station
5 St Joseph's convent
6 Archaeological museum
7 Acropolis of Kitionnn
8 Tennis courts
9 Phoenician temple
10 Mycenean walls
11 Market
12 Mycenean site
13 Hospital
14 Customs house
15 Park and zoo
16 Library
17 Telephones
18 Stadium
19 Central market
20 Cultural centre
21 Medieval fort (museum)
22 Phaneromeni
23 St Lazarus
1 Kyriakos
2 Makris
3 Acropolis
1 EMAN
2 to Paralimni
3 Ayios Lazaros Sq

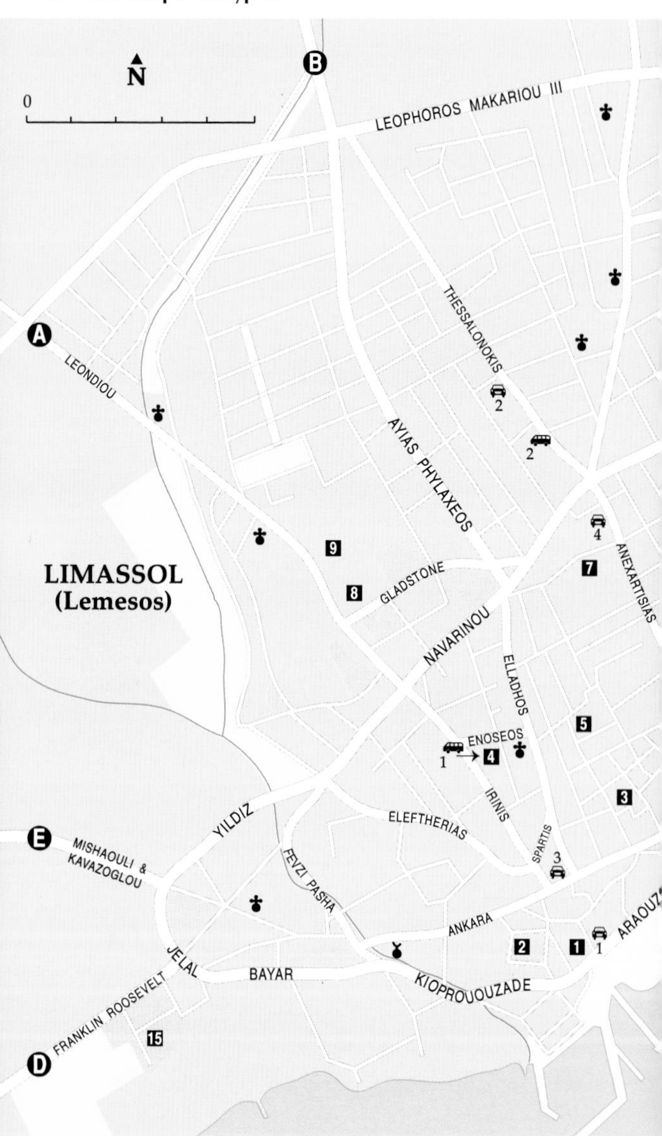

LIMASSOL (LEMESOS)

1 Tourist information
2 Castle and museum
3 Town hall
4 Bishop's seat
5 Market
6 Telephones
7 Administration offices
8 Police headquarters
9 Hospital
10 Library
11 Stadium
12 Zoo and public gardens
13 Theatre
14 Archaeological museum
15 Distillery
🚗1 Kypros, Acropolis
🚗2 Karydas, Kyriakos
🚗3 Makris
🚗4 Nea Paphos
🚌1 Kemek, Kallenos, Agros
🚌2 Costas Bus Co

AYIA (AGIA) NAPA

1 Tourist information & Cyprus Airways
2 Post office
3 Telephones
4 Monastery
5 Police station
6 Bus station

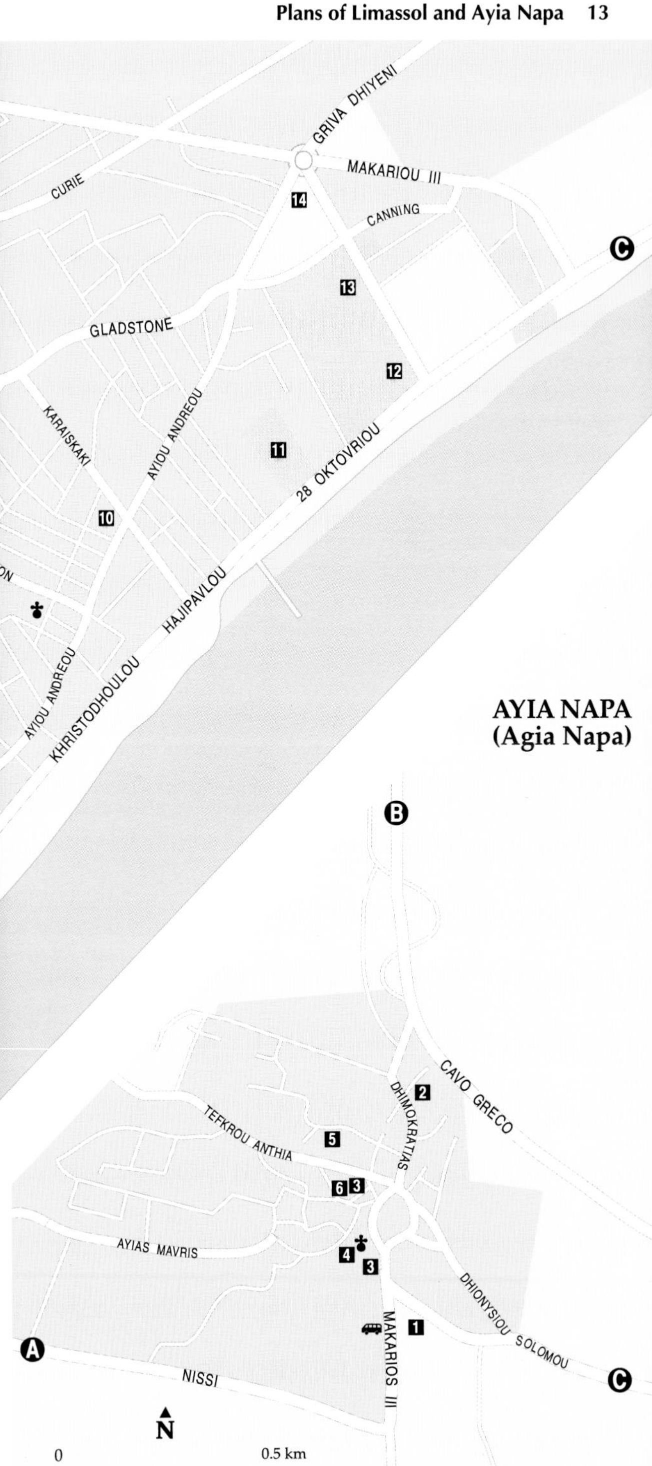
GRIVA DHIYENI
MAKARIOU III
CURIE
CANNING
GLADSTONE
KARAISKAKI
AYIOU ANDREOU
28 OKTOVRIOU
HAJIPAVLOU
KHRISTODHOULOU
AYIOU ANDREOU
14
13
12
11
10
C
AYIA NAPA
(Agia Napa)
B
CAVO GRECO
DHIMOKRATIAS
TEFKROU ANTHIA
AYIAS MAVRIS
DHIONYSIOU SOLOMOU
MAKARIOS III
NISSI
A
C
N
0
0.5 km

Picnicking

Picnicking is great fun on Cyprus, not least for Cypriots themselves, who will happily tuck into an outdoor feast, especially at weekends or on festival days. This enthusiasm does not extend to walking for pleasure, however, so you are most likely to come across groups of local families enjoying an outing at an official site which is easily accessible by car.

Such a site might suit your requirements — or you may prefer to seek out somewhere much more secluded along the route of a walk. Much of the island is open countryside, but it is a matter of common sense and courtesy not to picnic within any obvious fencing or boundary.

Official sites: The Cyprus Tourism Organisation and Forestry Department have established some 27 sites. Most of them are concentrated in the Troodos mountain region, but there is an excellent site near Polis, north of Paphos, close to several walks and car tours described in this book. The best sites offer car parking, toilet facilities, drinking water, tables and benches, barbecue facilities and play areas for children. At some of the smaller sites in less visited areas, facilities might be minimal. Official sites are indicated in the car touring notes and on the fold-out touring map by the symbol (⛩). Remember that in winter and early spring many will be inaccessible, since they lie along rough mountain roads. A leaflet describing all these sites and a few official camp sites (the only places where camping is allowed) is available from tourist information centres on the island.

Alternative suggestions: If you prefer a picnic 'away from it all', or if you find official sites crowded (likely at weekends and in high summer), you could picnic along one of the walks in this book.

All the information you need to get to one of these 'private' picnics is given on the following pages, *where picnic numbers correspond to walk numbers,* so that you can quickly find the general location by looking at the pull-out touring map (on which the area of each walk is shown by a white outline). I include transport details (🚌: how to get there by bus; 🚗: where to park if you come by car or taxi), how long a walk you'll have each way, and views or setting. Beside the picnic title you'll find a map reference: the exact location of the picnic spot is shown on this *walking* map by the symbol ***P***. Finally, to help you choose the right setting, many of the picnic spots are illustrated.

Please remember that these 'alternative' picnic places are generally off the beaten track: you will need to wear sensible shoes and almost certainly a sunhat (the symbol ○ at the right of a picnic title indicates a *picnic place in full sun*).

If travelling to your picnic by service taxi or bus, please be sure to collect an up-to-date transport timetable, with operators' telephone numbers.

If travelling to your picnic by hired car, watch out for animals and children on country roads and drive especially carefully through narrow village streets. Do park well off the road — without damaging plants — and *never* block a road or track.

All picnickers should read the country code on page 19 and go quietly in the countryside.

1 MOUNT OLYMPUS (map pages 54-55, photograph page 49)

by car: 45min on foot *by bus and taxi: 45min on foot*

🚗: park on Troodos main street (8km north of Platres).

🚐: take a minibus or taxi from Limassol to Platres, then go on to Troodos by local taxi.

From Troodos, follow Walk 1 along the Atalante trail for the first 3km, to an open area where there are numerous picnicking possibilities in pleasant surroundings and with extensive views. On the Artemis Trail (the Alternative walk) there are numerous benches with stunning views where picnics can be enjoyed.

2 MAKRYA KONTARKA (map pages 54-55, photograph page 51)

by car: 10-50min on foot *by bus and taxi: 10-50min on foot*

🚗 and 🚐: as Picnic 1 above

From Troodos, take the nature trail from the southern end of the main street as described in Walk 2 for under 10 minutes, to the group of benches among tall pines shown on page 51. This is a cool spot, but a picnic at the end of the trail (Makrya Kontarka), with magnificent views — similar to those on page 60 — is highly recommended, although there is little shade.

3 CALEDONIAN FALLS (map pages 54-55, photograph page 53)

by car: 5-45min on foot *by bus: not practical*

🚗: park near the southern end of the Caledonian Falls nature trail, by the side of a rough road that leads from a point slightly west of the trout farm (see map for car symbol). From here it's a five minute walk to the falls (signposted). Alternatively, park at the start of the nature trail (see Walk 3, page 53) and follow the walk to the falls, or find a suitable place to sit within a shorter distance.

Shady trees and pleasant ferns characterise this picnic spot.

4 MESAPOTAMOS (map pages 54-55, photograph page 57)

by car: up to 5min on foot *by bus and taxi: up to 5min on foot*

: park at Mesapotamos Monastery: rough roads lead from Platres or Saittas to this disused retreat.

: take a minibus from Limassol to Platres, then go on by local taxi (be sure to arrange your return).

This is a wooded setting with good shade. There is an official site nearby, but there's also scope for quieter outings.

5 THE MULE TRAIL (map pages 54-55)

by car or taxi: 1h10min on foot *by bus and taxi: 1h10min on foot*

or as Picnic 1 above. Follow Walk 5 for 1h10min, to the green bench at the start of the mule trail.

Excellent views southwards from your vantage point. On your return, take a different route back to Troodos: at the junction 10 minutes back from the bench, keep straight ahead instead of bearing right.

7 MADHARI RIDGE (map page 62, photograph page 62)

by car: 15-40min on foot *by bus: not practical*

: park near the start of the nature trail described in Walk 7.

From the nature trail arch, climb to the bench at the 15min-point for a short walk offering superb views over Kyperounda village; or follow Walk 7 for about 40 minutes, to the clearing with views over the Mesaoria Plain and towards Mt Adelphi.

9 MT TRIPYLOS (map page 66)

by car: 40min on foot *by bus: not practical*

: park at the Dhodheka Anemi junction (the 53km-point in Car tour 3, page 29), or see Walk 9, page 65.

Look for the gated track (from which vehicles are now barred) on the right, signposted to Mt Tripylos and follow it for 2km to the peak (1362m/4470ft), from where there are magnificent views. At the top you'll see a fire-watch station and a small picnic area which couldn't have a lovelier setting!

House of mystery: this farmhouse, abandoned for 60 years (see page 80), is one of the settings for Picnic 16. Nearby is a rusting threshing machine.

.ooking west from the monks' cemetery at Stavrovouni Monastery vhere photography, regrettably, is no longer permitted (Picnic 26).

11 MAVROKOLYMBOS DAM (map page 70)

)y car: up to 15min on foot *by bus: not practical*
: park near the dam (the rough road is signposted off the main Paphos-Coral Bay road.
About 2.5km from the main road you'll find a quiet spot on the banks of this irrigation reservoir.

13 LARA BEACH (map pages 98-99, photos pages 72-73 and 97) ○

)y car or boat: up to 10min on foot *by bus: not accessible*
: park at Lara Beach or take a from Paphos (see Walk 13, page 72).
A quiet undeveloped beach with a single, seasonal taverna.

16 ALEKHTORA (map page 82, photograph opposite)

)y car: up to 45 min on foot *by bus: not practical*
: park well off the road near the packing depot at the start of Walk 16 page 79).
Follow Walk 16 to the Khapotami Gorge overlook and find a convenient spot to picnic (about 40min), or keep west on the cobbled track at the 25min-point, to go straight to the farmhouse shown opposite (45min).

8 'APHRODONIS' TRAIL (map on reverse of touring map, photographs pages 84, 85, 87)

)y car: up to 1h on foot *by bus and taxi: up to 1h on foot*
: park at the tourist pavilion at the Baths of Aphrodite.
from Paphos to Polis; then take a taxi to the Baths.
Walk the shared early part of the Aphrodite and Adonis nature trails described in Walk 18 for up to 1h (numerous benches and viewpoints).

9 SMIYIES (map on reverse of touring map)

)y car: up to 40min on foot *by bus and taxi: up to 40min on foot*
: park on the edge of Neokhorio (as for Walk 19, page 88)
from Paphos to Polis; then take a taxi to Neokhorio.
A well-sited picnic area, with water, tables and benches. There are several short walk opportunities in the immediate vicinity.

26 STAVROVOUNI (map page 105, photos pages 17 and 105) ○

by car: 5min on foot *by bus: not practica*

🚗: park just below the monastery.

From the top of this striking pedestal you have a panoramic view o Cyprus. Women are not allowed in the monastery, but views from th car park are equally impressive. Toilets; sometimes a fruit stall.

27 EAST OF AYIA NAPA (map pages 108-109, photographs pages 106-107 and below) ○

by car: 5-40min on foot *by bus: 15-40min on foo*

🚗: park at Ayia Napa near the start of Walk 27 (see page 106).

🚌: check Ayia Napa region times and routes at a tourist office.

The early stages of Walk 27 offer numerous picnic opportunities, th best sand being at Kermia Beach (no shade). Head straight there by ca if you do not wish to walk.

28 AYII SARANTA (map map pages 108-109, cover photograph)

by car: 20min on foot *by bus: not practica*

🚗: park short of the transmitter tower, then walk round to Ayii Sarant (2km; 45min return) as described in Short walk 28 on page 111.

A pleasant location in the shadow of the unusual little church show on the cover, set on a hill in the quiet agricultural area inland from th lively resort of Ayia Napa.

Looking to Cape Greco from Ayia Napa (Picnic 27)

A country code for walkers and motorists

The experienced rambler is accustomed to following a 'country code' on his walks, but the tourist out for a lark can unwittingly cause damage, harm animals and even endanger his own life. A code for behaviour based on self-discipline is important wherever people are free to roam over the countryside, and doubly so on rugged terrain. On Cyprus, special care should be taken to avoid fires.

Do not light fires, except in the areas provided at official picnic sites. Never allow children to play with matches. Never throw cigarette ends away in the forest. If you see a fire in or near a forest, put it out if you can. If you cannot, use the nearest telephone (T on our maps) to inform the police or Forestry Department.

Do not frighten animals. By making loud noises or trying to touch or photograph them, you may cause them to run in fear and be hurt.

Leave all gates just as you found them. Although animals may not be in evidence, the gates do have a purpose; generally they keep grazing or herded sheep or goats in — or out of — an area.

Protect all wild and cultivated plants. Leave them in place for others to enjoy. Flowers will die before you get them back to your hotel; fruit is obviously someone's livelihood. ***Never walk over cultivated ground.***

Take all your litter away with you.

Do not block roads or tracks. Park where you will not inconvenience anyone or cause danger.

Walkers: *do not take risks!* Don't attempt walks beyond your capacity. Remember that there is very little twilight on Cyprus ... nor are there any officially-organised rescue services. If you were to injure yourself, it might be a very long time before you are found.

Do *not* walk alone, and *always* tell a responsible person exactly where you are going and what time you plan to return. On any but a very short walk near to villages, be sure to carry a compass, whistle, torch, an extra woollie and plenty of water and high-energy food like chocolate.

Touring

Driving on the roads of Cyprus (keep to the left) can be great pleasure, but it does at times call for the ability t resist impatience. It can also be tiring in the hot sun. S do not aim for long distances. Better to really *enjoy* shorter run than simply clock up kilometres. Punctuat days out in the car with short walks and relaxing picnics

My touring notes are brief: they include little history o information that can be gleaned from leaflets availabl free at all tourist centres and pavilions. Instead, I concen trate on the logistics of touring: road conditions, view points, distances, and good places to rest. Most of all, emphasise possibilities for **walking** and **picnicking** (th symbol ***P*** alerts you to a picnic spot; see pages 14-18) While some of the walk suggestions may not be suitabl for a long car tour, you may discover a landscape yo would like to explore at leisure another day.

The tours (which include 4WD suggestions) radiat from the three main tourist centres: Paphos, Limassol an

The hot Cyprus sun can do strange things to one's body. Here at Nissi Beach, as afternoon shadows lengthen, these sunseekers are oblivious to the way they look after hours of trying to achieve a golden-brown, all-over tan. Very easy to do at Nissi, but don't stay too long. Meanwhile, the fellow at the top obviously has a touch of sunstroke. He thinks he has scored with a beach beauty. But don't squeeze too hard, friend, or the lady will go to pieces...

arnaca. Bearing in mind that Cyprus is the third largest sland in the Mediterranean — some 222 kilometres (138 niles) from east to west — do not plan to tour the *entire* sland without an overnight stop or two!

The large touring map is designed to be held out oppo-ite the touring notes and contains all the information you vill need outside the towns (town plans with exit routes eyed to the touring map are on pages 8 to 13).

Make sure your **car is in good condition**: keep a regular heck on tyres, brakes, water, oil and lights. Always carry varm clothing (especially in the mountains, even in ummer) in case of delays or breakdowns. Allow plenty of time for **stops**: my times include only short breaks at iewpoints labelled (📷) in the touring notes. **Telephones** in green kiosks) are located in towns and most villages, near post offices, but most bars and cafes will allow you o make a local call if necessary. **WCs** are available in arger centres; others are found in bars and cafes. **Distances** quoted are *cumulative* kilometres from the tarting point. A key to the **symbols** in the notes is on the ouring map.

All motorists should read the country code on page 19 and respect the environment.

1 WESTERN WAYS

Paphos • Coral Bay • Peyia • Kathikas • Drousha • Prod hromi • Lachi • Baths of Aphrodite • (4WD options) • Polis • Skoulli • Stroumbi • Paphos

115km/71mi; about 3h30min driving; leave Paphos on the road to th Tomb of the Kings (Exit D)

On route: ⊼ at Smiyies (4WD Route A); Picnics (see pages 14-18) 11 13, 18, 19; Walks 10-14, 17-23

A leisurely full-day tour on good metalled roads which are narrow an twisting in places. If you've hired a jeep for the first time, either of th suggestions on page 24 offers a good introduction to the joys of rough track driving! Both 4WD routes make shorter circuits than the full ca tour — about 80km in each case.

Leave Paphos on the road to the Tomb of the Kings (Exi D), at the traffic light junction between Paphos and Nea Paphos, just north of the Apollo Hotel. At 13km pas a signposted turning to the right — a rough track to Mavro kolymbos Dam (***P***11); it's on the route of Walk 11 fron Kissonerga. At 14km reach **Coral Bay★** (⛰✕📷), the popular beach and resort area shown on pages 68-69 where Walk 11 ends. If you need petrol, head about 1km or so towards Ayios Yeoryios, where you will find a station (⛽) on the right... and behind it, one of two reptile display centres on Cyprus.

From Coral Bay, head inland to **Peyia** (18km ✝✕📷) a large, cheerful, non-touristy village set on a hillside. As you climb beyond it, the views (📷) over the coas become at first appealing and then magnificent as you head for **Kathikas** (27km), which means 'perched on a hill'. Walk 12 sets off from the Visitors' Centre here created by the Laona Project for restoring villages in the Akamas to economic independence (see page 71).

Through Kathikas, there's an option to cross the main road and detour a few kilo-

The abandoned village of Theletra, an optional detour on the main car tour route beyond Skoulli.

metres to Pano and Kato Akourdhalia, two small Laona villages (combined population 100!) noted for springtime almond blossom, a herb garden, folk museum, excellent taverna/guest-house project, and the 12th-century church of Ayia Paraskevi.

Our route bears left at the main road for a few minutes, then turns left at a signpost through **Pano** and **Kato Arodhes** (32km), **Inia** (34km) and the larger village of **Drousha** (36km ; Walk 22), with its splendid views round the compass on a clear day. Come to the main road again, and turn left to continue the tour — or first turn right briefly, then left, at a signpost to Kritou Terra, from where there is a short and very pretty walk to Terra and back (see Walk 21 and photograph page 93).

Continuing north from Drousha on the main route, come to the coast road at **Prodhromi** and turn left to reach the fishing harbour and resort area of **Lachi** (50km). Lachi is the starting point for Walks 20 and 23; its colourful harbour is shown on page 91. Some 7km further on is the tourist pavilion at the **Baths of Aphrodite★** (Loutra Aphroditis; ***P***18), where Walks 17, 18 and Alternative walk 20-1 converge (see photographs pages 84-87).

Returning on the same road, those with 4WD vehicles may choose one of the options described on the next page, via Neokhorio, but if you are in a normal hire car you should come back through Lachi (64km) and Prodhromi to **Polis** (68km), an appealing town of ancient origin, and once centre of a thriving copper mining industry.

4WD OPTIONS

After visiting the Baths of Aphrodite, head back towards Lachi, but make a right turn and drive 3km to the village of **Neokhorio** (see reverse of touring map; normal hire cars can follow this stretch as well, but will need to return the same way). Drive carefully through the narrow, winding streets, passing the church on your right, and emerge at the other side of the village. Once clear of houses you will come to a fork in the road...

Route A is signposted to **Smiyies** and is a rough but level road leading in about 3km past the church of Ayios Minas to the Smiyies picnic site (⛩***P***19), a well-equipped and popular location where nature trails start and finish (see Walk 19). A well-shod hire car could make it this far but definitely ***no further***!

Drive past the picnic site (on your right) and head for the T-junction on the skyline. Turn left, then, after a short distance, turn right in the direction of Koudounas (signposted). Keep going for just under 3km to another junction, where you again turn right towards Koudounas. This rough track (and it *is* rough!) winds westward toward the coast road which you reach some 6km beyond the T-junction at Smiyies. The views are wonderful.

Turn left and drive about 7km to **Lara Beach** (Walk 13; photographs pages 72-73, 97). The track is rutted, but gives access to a number of secluded beaches where you could skinny-dip with impunity, or picnic to your heart's content.

From Lara, continue on the rough track, past the signposted Viklari taverna on your left and the turn-off to the Avagas Gorge (Walk 14; photograph page 74). After 6km come into **Ayios Yeoryios**, where the road becomes metalled.

From Ayios Yeoryios, where there is a small harbour, rock tombs and a church of 6th century origin, you have a simple drive of about 20km to Paphos, via Coral Bay and Kissonerga.

Route B follows Route A to the fork beyond **Neokhorio**. Here turn left past a goat enclosure and drive for 5km to the semi-ruined village of **Androlikou** (Walks 20 and 23; photograph page 92). This was once Turkish, but is now occupied by only one Greek family and hundreds of goats, plus a flock of sheep, a few pigs and vigilant but harmless dogs. Come into the village and turn right to head for **Fasli**, about 3km distant, which is completely abandoned. Walk 23 comes this way; you may like to refer to the map on pages 98-99. At a ridge 1km beyond Fasli, where a left turn would take you to Drousha, turn right along an appallingly rutted track for 1km, then turn left to gain wonderful views over the coastline. This track takes you to the coast road, just above **Lara Beach**. From here the return to Paphos is as described in Route A.

From top to bottom: disused spring at Kato Arodhes; farmer at Akoursos; poppies and daisies; giant fennel (Ferula communis), *most commonly seen on the Akamas Peninsula*

From here follow the signposted main road back towards Paphos, with optional short stops and detours. At **Skoulli** (78km), the Herpetological Society of Cyprus operates the second reptile exhibition on this tour. You may not be fond of these creatures but it's useful to know what they look like!

A right turn at about 86km offers a detour to Miliou, a tiny Laona village noted for traditional weaving, and a few kilometres further on, a similar right turn leads to the totally abandoned village of Theletra, where the threat of landslips caused mass evacuation almost 20 years ago. It's an atmospheric place to explore, but keep to the streets — the crumbling buildings could be unsafe.

Pass through **Stroumbi** (98km ✕) to reach **Mesoyi** (108km), from where a right turn would take you to the monastery of Ayios Neophytos (✝📷; Walk 10) — an optional detour of 8km return. From Mesoyi, it's a short drive back to the centre of **Paphos** (115km), after a day spent exploring a varied and unhurried region of the island.

2 OLD VILLAGES, ROCKS AND BONES!

Paphos • Yeroskipos • Kouklia • Pano Arkhimandrita • Dhora • Arsos • Omodhos • Episkopi • Kourion • Petra tou Romiou • Paphos

130km/81mi; about 3h30min driving; Exit A from Paphos

On route: Picnic (see pages 14-18) 16; Walks 15 and 16

A full day's tour, packed with variety and interesting scenery — mostly on good metalled roads (but sometimes on terrible ones!)

Head out of Paphos on the Limassol road (Exit A; Leophoros Yeoryiou Griva Dhiyeni). The first village, effectively a suburb of Paphos, is **Yeroskipos** (3km ✝🏛✕⛽**M**), renowned for *loukoumi,* the delicacy shown on page 30. Call it Turkish delight if you wish, but not within Greek earshot. One of only two surviving five-domed Byzantine churches on Cyprus stands here, Ayia Paraskevi. (The other, at Peristerona, is visited on Car tour 5; see drawing on pages 44-45). Also of interest is the Folk Art Museum: housed in an 18th-century building, it holds an impressive collection of implements both domestic and agricultural, plus rural apparel.

Pass the airport turn-off at **Timi** and, beyond **Mandria** (⛽), turn left to **Koukliaâ˜…** (16km **π**✕**M**), site of the Temple of Aphrodite and Ancient ('Palea') Paphos. It is likely that old Paphos was destroyed by earthquakes in the 12th century BC, and there is little for the casual visitor to see, but the temple and nearby medieval manor are impressive.

Drive slowly through Kouklia. Then a tortuous road takes you to **Pano Arkhimandrita** (30km). Walk 15 (an all-time favourite with 'Landscapers') starts here, and it is worthwhile to pause for a short time to visit the shrine of Ayii Pateres (see illustration page 75) and view the scenery which is spectacular on all sides and brilliantly green in springtime, as the photograph on pages 76-77 testifies.

The road continues on a rougher surface through tiny **Mousere** and skirts round **Dhora** (37km), to a junction (44km). Turn left and follow the sign to **Arsos** (48km), noted for its dark red wine. Enter the village if you wish, or simply follow the 'bypass', which brings you to a clear sign indicating a right turn onto a rough road to **Omodhos** (60km ✝✕**M**). This larger village, too, is famed for the quality of its wine, and is well worth exploring. The pedestrianised central area is a touch commercial, but you have to buy your wine, *soujoukko, loukoumi,* lace, postcards, olive oil and terracotta pots somewhere, so why not here? Be sure to wander the narrow streets, too, and observe how exquisitely restored many of the houses

Papa Louka, the priest at Pano Arkhimandrita, and a wall painting inside his church

are. The central Monastery of Stavros is modern but worth inspecting.

On the far side of Omodhos, turn left on a fast road signposted to Limassol, passing turn-offs to Pakhna, Ayios Amvrosios, Pano Kividhes and Kandou, before hitting the coast road and turning right to drive through **Episkopi** (83km ✕⛽**M**). This is the centre of the British military presence on Cyprus, one of two Sovereign Base Areas — the other being at Dhekelia, east of Larnaca (Car tour 7).

Just beyond Episkopi is the ancient site of **Kourion★** (**Π**✕📷), one of the most important excavations on the island (open daily). Visit the tourist pavilion and acquire all the information you need to make the most of your visit to Kourion and the nearby **Temple of Apollo★** (**Π**). Then continue east above Pissouri, from where you could make a detour to Alekhtora (***P***16), either to picnic or to enjoy a short walk overlooking the Khapotami Gorge.

Our last visit for today is to the famed **Rocks of Aphrodite★** (103km ✕), where Walk 16 ends. There is a tourist pavilion for your refreshment and enlightenment. It is said that the Goddess of Love was born from the sea foaming against the offshore rocks here (of which **Petra tou Romiou** is one; 'petra' means stone). From the rocks, Aphrodite was carried by a shell to the shore — a story most vividly illustrated in Botticelli's painting, *The Birth of Venus.*

Not far beyond Aphrodite's rocks is the Kouklia turn-off where we started up into the hills earlier in the day. From here it's a straight run back to **Paphos** (130km).

3 LAND OF THE MOUFFLON

Paphos • Polemi • Kannaviou • Stavros tis Psokas • Dhodheka Anemi • Cedar Valley • Kykko Monastery • Panayia • Chrysorroyiatissa Monastery • Statos • Paphos

approximately 140km/87mi; about 4h driving; Exit B from Paphos

On route: ⛩ on the easier track between Kannaviou and Stavros, Stavros Forestry Station, Cedar Valley; Picnic (see pages 14-18) 9; Walks 8, 9

A full day's tour, partly on rough mountain roads, packed with variety and beautiful landscapes. Allow plenty of time. A 4WD vehicle would find the challenge easier, but you can also do this trip in a well-shod standard hire car if you follow the easier track to Stavros.

Take Exit B from Paphos (Leophoros Evagora Pallikaridis). Some 13km out of town, make a right turn (signposted) to **Polemi** (16km), a large grape-packing community, and from here continue to **Kannaviou** (24km ✕).

About 1.5km beyond Kannaviou, turn left on an unsurfaced road which forks after less than 1km. Both of these routes lead to **Stavros tis Psokas** (43km ▲⛩). But the track on the left should really only be considered by 4WD users, especially in winter or early spring. The scenery is truly spectacular, but the way is rough. Those of you in normal hire cars would be better advised to use the other, easier route, via the Agia picnic site. It is less demanding but still beautiful.

Stavros is named after a monastery originally sited here, called Stavros tis Psoras (Cross of the Measles); the spring at Stavros reputedly held holy water which cured

that illness. The forests around Stavros are home to the timid moufflon, but you are more likely to see examples in captivity at the forest station.

From Stavros continue uphill, observing on the right the start of the Horteri Nature Trail (Walk 8), and come to a road junction with comprehensive signposting. On the left is another short nature trail ('Moutti tou Stavrou', also described in Walk 8). Turn right here towards Kykko and come after about 8km to a junction at **Dhodheka Anemi** (53km ***P***9). Park here for a moment and consider walking the 4km to **Mt Tripylos** and back, to break up your day. The views from this peak (1362m/4470ft) are magnificent. Walk 9 offers a long, but fairly easy circuit in this area.

The road straight ahead leads to Kykko Monastery after 17km, but it is more scenic to take the signposted forest road to the right — to **Cedar Valley★** (63km ⊼), a lovely remote region of tall, majestic cedars. This links up again with our original route and comes to a surfaced north/south road, where we turn right to **Kykko Monastery★** (82km ✝⛪), famed throughout the Greek Orthodox world and one of the biggest landowners on Cyprus. Kykko has an interesting history both ancient and recent; it contains, among other treasures, an icon attributed to St Luke.

About 1.5km west of Kykko, a steep road leads up to **Throni★** (📷), the mountain-top tomb of Archbishop

Painting (left) and wall mosaic at Kykko. The monastery is almost sumptuous in its decor, compared with more humble retreats.

Market stalls: Loukoumi (left); fruits and nuts

Makarios, from where the views are superb. On your descent turn right and follow the track for 11km — to the first fork, where you should turn right. Turn left after 3km at the next fork, and left again after another 5km, to come to **Panayia** (108km), the birthplace of Makarios, where you meet surfaced road.

Beyond Panayia, you have three options for your return to Paphos. You can continue on the good road through Asproyia to Kannaviou, from there retracing the outward journey. But you may wish to see **Chrysorroyiatissa Monastery★** (✝☗📷), only 1.5km from Panayia. From the monastery head south to **Statos**, then *either* proceed via Pendalia, Nata and Anarita to the coast road at Timi (opposite the airport turn-off) and turn right; *or* head for the Paphos-Polis road via Khoulou, Kourdaka and Tsadha. Each of the three options brings you back to **Paphos** (140km) after a perhaps tiring but spectacular day in high and holy places.

4 FROM PAPHOS TO PLATRES

Paphos • Asprokremnos Dam • Nikouklia • Phasoula • Ayios Yeoryios • Kithasi • Kedhares • Ayios Nikolaos • Kato Platres • Pano Platres

approximately 60km/37mi; about 1h30min driving; Exit A from Paphos

On route: A around Troodos (see map pages 54-55); Picnics (see pages 14-18) 1-5; Walks 1-6

An easy but pretty drive from Paphos through a picturesque river valley into the Troodos foothills, where you can link up with Car tour 5 if you wish to continue to Nicosia, and a choice of return routes to Paphos.

It's a lot easier that it once was to reach the Troodos Mountains from Paphos. There is still no *fast* way of doing it, but who wants one?

This is arguably the most direct route, and it is certainly an attractive morning's drive. Leave Paphos at Exit A on the Limassol road, and take the first major left turn after the airport turn-off. It is signposted to **Asprokremnos Dam**, which is reached at about 14km. This is one of the larger (and newer) reservoirs on the island, and you should cross the dam wall very slowly, because the speed-reducing ramps are quite severe. Turn left on the far side and come to **Nikouklia**.

You are in the beautiful Dhiarizos Valley shown below, and you may observe the abandoned village of Souskiou across the river (which may be bone dry late in the year). At **Phasoula** (25km), you may care to look at the mosque shown overleaf.

Proceed very easily through **Ayios Yeoryios**, **Kithasi** and **Kedhares** to **Ayios Nikolaus** (44km) which offers a choice of tavernas and some lovely views westward over the upper Dhiarizos Valley.

After leaving Ayios Nikolaus, start to get impressive views of the Troodos Mountains. Continue through **Mandria** and **Kato** (lower) **Platres** to reach **Pano** (upper) **Platres★** (▲✕⛽📷⊕) at about 60km. This mountain resort has all the facilities you could want, and nearby are

Left: in the Dhiarizos Valley; soft-top 4WD vehicles are an ideal way of exploring Cyprus.

several walk options (***P***1-5; Walks 1-6; see area map pages 54-55 and photographs pages 49-61).

You can now follow Car tour 5 for a run of about 80km via Troodos to **Nicosia** on good metalled roads. But there are several appealing options for a return drive to Paphos.

Option 1: Follow the early section of Car tour 5 in reverse from Platres to Limassol (about 40km), then it's another 72km along the coast road back to Paphos.

Option 2: Retrace your route as far as Mandria, then follow signs to Omodhos, from where you can drive part of Car tour 2 in reverse — via Mallia, Dhora, and Pano Arkhimandrita. When you reach the coast road at Kouklia, return to Paphos (about 130km in total).

Option 3: For a really full day's sightseeing, set off early from Paphos to Platres and Troodos, then drive via Prodhromos and Pedhoulas to Kykko Monastery, and follow Car tour 3 for a return to Paphos, making a splendid 'Grand Tour' of around 150km covering the west of the island.

Top: As an alternative to jeeps, you can get around the island by bus (Troodos, top left; Drousha, right), bicycle, or on horseback (Platres). Left: disused mosque at Phasoula; right: church of St Michael the Archangel at Pedhoulas

5 A CAPITAL CIRCUIT

Limassol • Trimiklini • Platres • Troodos • Kakopetria • Galata • Peristerona • Nicosia • (Stavrovouni) • Limassol

approximately 200km/125 mi; about 4-5h driving; Exit A from Limassol

On route: ⛩ at Platania and Passia's Meadow (both north of Troodos towards Kakopetria on the west side of the road), also Kornos Forestry Station a few miles from Stavrovouni; Picnics (see pages 14-18) 1, 3, 4, 7, 26; Walks 1-7, 24, 26. (Walk 25 is also best reached from Limassol.)

A long circuit with many optional detours. Quite easy to accomplish in one day if you like driving, but impossible if you want to do a lot of exploring. It makes an excellent two-day outing with an overnight stay in Nicosia. All roads are metalled.

Driving in Limassol (its new name is Lemesos, by the way) is not for the faint-hearted! The town's traffic management leaves much to be desired and one should especially be wary of kamikaze moped riders. But here is an escape from such urban perils. Leave the bustling environs of Limassol at the Polemidhia roundabout (Exit A; junction with Makarios Avenue) and follow the Platres and Troodos sign. The road, still narrow in places, has been much improved to allow comparatively swift transit from the coast to the mountains in barely an hour. Pass Polemidhia Dam on your left after a few kilometres, reaching **Trimiklini** (30km ✕).

After Trimiklini, swing left at the Saittas turn-off (***P***4), passing Moniatis before coming into **Platres**★ (37km ▲✕⛽📷⊕). This resort is fragmented around the pine-clad hillsides at an invigorating altitude of 1100m/3600ft. Park awhile, and at least explore the central area where you will find shops, banks and a tourist information office. You may also care to look at the Forest Park Hotel, where Daphne Du Maurier wrote the novel *Rebecca*.

You might turn to pages 54-55 before resuming your journey. It is obvious from this 1:50,000 scale map of the Troodos region that Platres is an excellent centre for walkers (especially those with a hire car) and there are many hotels in the area, of all categories. Walks 3, 4 and 5 finish in the centre near the Tourist Information Office; Walk 6 is a short drive away.

From Platres the tour continues up to the trout farm (and ***P***3) to **Troodos** (45km ▲✕⛽📷***P***1), which is virtually one street. The air is pine-fresh and you are just 3-4km from the summit of Mount Olympus★ (Π📷) to the northwest, one of the optional detours on this tour. This is the highest point on Cyprus, at 1952m/6400ft. The island's short skiing season (January to March) is centred on its slopes; there is also a radar installation, a TV mast and the

The priest at Nikitari holds the keys to this church at Asinou, the finest Byzantine church on Cyprus. Murals cover the interior.

remains of a Venetian tower. Walk 1 is a lovely way of experiencing Mount Olympus.

From Troodos, Walk 2 is an easy leg-stretcher and offers splendid views to the northeast and the route we are about to cover. The road sweeps past the Pano Amiandos mine on the right and the turn-off to Kyperounda (***P***7; Walk 7). You will see two official picnic sites to the left (⛩) before coming into **Kakopetria** (60km✝⛰✕⛽ and ✝ Ayios Nikolaos 3km southwest) and **Galata** (64km ✝⛰✕) — foothill villages which both reward exploration if you have the time, especially if you enjoy old churches.

This route goes via **Peristerona** (85km; see notes and illustration pages 44-45), but consider first a 28km return detour to Asinou church★ (shown above) from the Koutraphas crossroads, via Nikitari. Through Peristerona, head straight for **Nicosia (Lefkosia)**★ (117km ✝✝⛰✕⛽⊕**ΠΤΜ**), the attractions, sights and peculiarities of which are fully detailed in tourist office material. If you are staying overnight, you might consider a brief crossing (on foot) into the Turkish-occupied area at the Ledra checkpoint, and you should certainly see the colourful Laiti Yitonia area near the city centre, the Venetian walls, the Cyprus Museum, and the ancient Cathedral of St John.

Leaving Nicosia on Archbishop Makarios Avenue (Exit A on the town plan on pages 8-9), reach the M1 dual carriageway for a swift return to Limassol in an hour or so. But a detour of about 18km (return) to Stavrovouni Monastery★ (Car tour 6; photographs pages 17, 105; Walk 26) is highly recommended. Other possible excursions off this route include the lace-making centre of Lefkara, but this could prove costly! The good people of Lefkara will do their utmost to persuade you to spend!

Before coming into **Limassol** you may care to dally at Governor's Beach (Walk 24), where there are facilities of a ramshackle nature, or call at the Monastery of Ayios Yeoryios Alamanou. Walk 24 starts at this distinctive blue and white retreat (shown on page 101), where the nuns sell flowers and a lone monk paints icons.

6 THE HEIGHT OF ORTHODOXY

Larnaca • Hala Sultan Tekke • Kiti • Dhromolaxia • Kalokhorio • Pyrga • Stavrovouni Monastery • Kophinou • Larnaca

approximately 100km/62mi; about 3h driving; Exit B from Larnaca

On route: ⛩ at the Kornos Forestry Station a few miles from Stavrovouni; Picnic (see pages 14-18) 26; Walk 26

A full day out from Larnaca, taking in a Moslem holy place, one of the finest churches on Cyprus and the pinnacle of Stavrovouni. All roads are metalled. ***Note: Women are not allowed to enter Stavrovouni, neither is photography permitted.***

Take the road south to the airport (Exit B) for the start of this compact tour, and notice the shimmering whiteness of the salt lake, which is exploited commercially in the summer months. In winter it rains and the lake fills up, becoming a refuge for thousands of flamingoes and other migratory birds.

Just past the airport, turn right to palm-shrouded **Hala Sultan Tekke★** (5km ✗), the third most important place of Moslem pilgrimage, after Mecca and Medina. It is a shrine revered as the burial place of the prophet Mohammed's aunt. Take off your shoes and go inside...

'Twas in the mid-7th century during an Arab raid on the island that Umm Haram, maternal aunt of the prophet, was travelling with her husband when she fell from her mule and broke her neck. She was buried at once 'in that fragrant spot'. The location, shown below, is indeed beautiful, with the mosque and its minaret surrounded by gardens and trees. It is as much frequented by tourists as pilgrims these days, and there is a restaurant nearby. Excavations to the west of the mosque have revealed the

Hala Sultan Tekke

Kiti church, Panayia Angeloktisos

site of a Bronze Age town and many historically valuable artefacts. After visiting the Tekke ... put your shoes on again and return to the main road, turning right to reach **Kiti** village (11km ✝✕), which is notable only for the church shown above — the magnificent Panayia Angeloktisos★ ('built by angels'). It houses the finest Byzantine mosaics on Cyprus. Come back on the same road as far as Meneou, then turn left to pass through **Dhromolaxia**, shortly reaching a crossroads, at which keep ahead to **Kalokhorio** (26km ✝). Head for **Ayia Anna**, then **Pyrga** (35km ✝✕).

Some 1.5km beyond Pyrga you will meet the old Nicosia/Limassol road (⊼ near the Kornos Forestry Station). Turn left and after another 1.5km find the signposted turn-off to Stavrovouni. The monastery is reached after an unprepossessing drive of 10km — past a quarry and an army camp (remember not to take photographs in this area). **Stavrovouni Monastery★** (48km ✝📷***P***26) is the goal of Walk 26. The views (see photographs pages 17 and 105) are astounding, and the approach is by way of a series of hairpin bends, but the road (once a rough track) is now metalled.

After your visit, follow the *old* Limassol road south as far as **Kophinou** (70km ✕), and then turn left for a straight run back to **Larnaca** (about 100km).

hiring a 4WD vehicle. The hills, valleys, gorges and wild coastline around places like Polis, Lachi, Drousha Kathikas and Lara are completely unspoiled and highly rewarding for the experienced walker. I have included a number of Akamas walks in this new edition, but some Akamas secrets are better discovered on an organised Land Rover tour, such as operated by the environmentally-sensitive ExAlt organisation of Paphos.

Basic accommodation may be available at some (but not all) of the island's monasteries, but bedding is *not* provided. No charge is made, but a donation on departure is appreciated. This privilege is really intended for Greek Orthodox pilgrims, and as a tourist, if you really want somewhere cheap to stay, it is more appropriate to seek out a room in a village. This is a great help to the fragile rural economy, and you will get a good deal and a cheap, authentic Cypriot meal.

Accommodation for a maximum of three nights is available at the **Stavros Forestry Station** (see page 63); book in advance (tel 06-332144 or 06-722338).

A highly satisfying way of exploring Cyprus on foot for the first time would be to **combine a week in the Troodos with a week on the coast**. That way, you would have time some of that sun, sand and brandy sour!

Walking in the Akamas upland region

Weather

The Cyprus climate is splendidly Mediterranean, with constant sunshine during much of the year, and with rainfall being confined to a fairly short and predictable winter, when temperatures remain at a pleasurable level.

The walker probably experiences Cyprus at its climatic best between March and early summer, when the countryside is a blaze of floral colour and the sun hot, but not unbearably so. September and October are good walking months too.

The high Troodos region is cold in winter (and can be so beyond Easter), with snow usually allowing skiing for about eight weeks on the slopes of Mount Olympus. Summer temperatures here can be high, but they are usually a few refreshing degrees cooler than on the coast and consistently cooler than in Nicosia, where the mercury can go above 38° C (100° F) for days on end!

Important: Anyone planning a walking trip early in the year should note that rainfall can turn dry tracts into streams and rivers. Moreover, there might still be snow in the mountains, making it impossible to follow some walks and tours.

AVERAGE TEMPERATURES

Month	Average air temperature Min °C	Min °F	Max °C	Max °F	Average sea temperature °C	°F	%age of days with sun
Jan	8.9	47.9	18.3	65	16.5	61.4	57
Feb	9.4	49	19.4	66.9	16.9	62.4	63
Mar	10	50	20.6	69.1	17.3	63.2	67
Apr	12.2	53.9	22.8	73.1	18.6	65.5	71
May	15.6	60.1	27.2	81	21.1	69.9	79
Jun	18.3	65	30	85.9	24	75.3	87
Jul	22.8	73.1	35.6	96	26	79.4	90
Aug	22.8	73.1	35.6	96	27.8	81.9	88
Sep	18.3	65	32.2	90	27.6	80	88
Oct	17.2	63	27.8	82	25.1	77	80
Nov	12.2	53.9	23.9	75	21.9	71.4	71
Dec	8.3	46.9	17.2	66	18.9	66.4	59

What to take

If you are already on Cyprus when you find this book and do not have items like a rucksack or walking boots, you can still enjoy a number of the easier walks, or you can buy some equipment in one of the sports shops. Please do not attempt the longer or more difficult walks without the proper equipment. For each walk described, the absolute minimum equipment is given. Do adjust the equipment according to the season; for instance, take a long-sleeved shirt and long trousers, as well as a sunhat, in summer months, and some cardigans and raingear on cooler days.

Where walking boots are prescribed, there is, unfortunately, no substitute. You will need to rely on their grip and ankle protection and, occasionally, their waterproof qualities. If you do wear shoes, make sure they have rubber soles, preferably of the Vibram or Skywalk variety. The often stony and dusty tracks of Cyprus can be unforgiving toward the improperly shod walker.

Bear in mind, if you would, that I have not done *all* the walks in this book under *all* weather conditions. I may not realise just how hot or how wet a walk can be, depending on the season.

Nevertheless, if you intend going to Cyprus properly kitted out, you may find the following checklist useful. I rely on your good judgment to modify your equipment according to circumstances and the season. It is always wise to seek out local advice about conditions before undertaking any walk, especially in the hills.

walking boots (which must be broken-in and comfortable)
waterproof gear (outside summer months)
torch (if only for inspecting the darkened interiors of ruined churches!)
long-sleeved shirt (for sun protection)
long trousers, tight at the ankles
small/medium-sized rucksack
up-to-date transport timetables
safety pins, string, clips
lightweight jacket
knives and openers
first aid kit
plastic groundsheet
plastic cups, plates, bottles
extra pairs of socks
anorak (zip opening)
2 lightweight cardigans
plastic rainhat
sunhat, suncream
extra bootlaces
whistle, compass
telephone numbers of taxi operators

Walkers' checklist

The following cannot be stressed too often:

- **NEVER walk alone** — four is the best walking group.
- **Do not overestimate your energy**. Your speed will be determined by the slowest walker in your group.
- **If a walk becomes unsafe**, do not try to press ahead.
- **Transport connections** at the end of a walk are very important.
- **Proper shoes** or boots are vital.
- **Always take a sunhat** with you, and in summer a cover-up for your arms and legs as well.

- **Warm clothing** is needed in the mountains, especially in case you are delayed.
- **Mists** can fall suddenly in the mountains.
- In spring, normally-dry **riverbeds may be flooded**.
- **Always carry water and rations** on long walks.
- **Compass, whistle, torch** weigh little, but could save your life.
- **A stout stick** is a help on rough terrain and to discourage the rare unfriendly dog.
- **Do not panic** in an emergency.
- **Re-read the important note** on page 2 and the guidelines on grade and equipment for each walk you do.

Nuisances

Thankfully there are few nuisances to worry about when walking on Cyprus, but some walkers might favour carrying a stick: this could be of help on gradients and in the vicinity of goat enclosures, which are often guarded by noisy **dogs**. The best solution is to keep your stick out of sight, only using it defensively if absolutely necessary.

It should be noted that poisonous **snakes** are indigenous to the island, along with non-venomous varieties (see page 6 under 'Books': *Nature of Cyprus*). The chances of an encounter are slim, as snakes are shy creatures. As a precaution, however, it is wise to check under rocks or logs (perhaps with your stick) before settling down for a picnic, especially if you are somewhere very hot, close to water.

Cyprus has hundreds of churches, ranging from tiny bare chapels in remote villages to ornately-decorated edifices containing priceless artefacts. You are likely to come upon long-ruined Byzantine churches with ages-old wall and ceiling paintings still visible. Many an old building is used by shepherds for shelter... for themselves or for their sheep and goats!

It is an unusual village that does not have a church of some kind. If the church is closed, and you would like to see inside it, ask at the local café, where they will readily raise the priest or caretaker, who will open the church for you. If you are exploring a place of worship, remember to dress in suitable clothing. It is also useful to carry a torch for the inspection of dark interiors.

Not every church is distinctive, but that of St Barnabas (Ayii Varnava) at Peristerona, shown here, certainly is. Its five-domed structure dates back to the 10th century, and there is only one other five-domed church on Cyprus — at Yeroskipos (Car tour 2).

There are mosques in Greek Cyprus, too, but almost all have remained closed since 1974 (a notable exception being Hala Sultan Tekke, of course: see Car tour 6).

Lizards of all shapes and sizes abound, but these are good fun!

Examples of all Cyprus reptiles, including snakes, are on view at the Herpetological Society's snake centre at Skoulli (near Polis on the road to Paphos) and at a similar centre between Coral Bay and Ayios Yeoryios (behind the BP station).

Photography

Photography is forbidden in some sensitive areas (eg near military bases or the 'green line'), but warning signs make any restrictions clear. Some museums and churches do not allow photography ... it is good manners to ask, in any case.

Greek for walkers

In the major tourist areas you hardly need to know any Greek at all, but once you are out in the countryside, a few words of the language will be helpful, and people will be grateful for your attempts to communicate.

Here's one way to ask directions in Greek and understand the answers you get! First memorise the few 'key' questions given below. Then, always follow up your key question with a second question demanding a yes ('ne') or no ('ochi') answer. Greeks invariably raise their heads to say 'no', which looks to us like the beginning of a 'yes'!

Following are the two most likely situations in which you may have to use some Greek. The dots (...) show

where you will fill in the name of your destination. I'd recommend that you purchase an inexpensive phrase book: many give easily-understood pronunciation hints, as well as a selection of phrases.

■ ASKING THE WAY

Key questions

English	*Approximate Greek pronunciation*
Good day, greetings	**Hair**-i-tay
Hello, hi (informal)	**Yas**-sas (plural); **Yia**-soo (singular)
Please — where is	**Sas** pa-ra-ka-**loh** — **pou ee**-nay
the road that goes to ...?	o **thro**-mo stoh ...?
the footpath that goes to ...?	ee mono-**pati** stoh ...?
the bus stop?	ee **sta**-ssis?
Many thanks.	Eff-hah-ree-**stoh** po-**li**.

Secondary question leading to a yes/no answer

Is it	**Ee**-nay
here?/there?/straight ahead?/	e-**tho**?/eh-**kee**?/kat-eff-**thia**?/
behind?/to the right?/	**pee**-so?/thex-**ya**?/
to the left?/above?/below?	aris-teh-**rah**?/eh-**pano**?/**kah**-to?

■ ASKING A TAXI DRIVER TO TAKE YOU/COLLECT YOU

Please —	**Sas** pa-ra-ka-**loh** —
would you take us to ...?	Tha **pah**-reh mas stoh ... ?
Come and pick us up	**El**-la na mas -reh-teh
from ... (place) at ... (time)*	apo ... stees ...*

*Point on your watch to the time you wish to be collected

Organisation of the walks

Each ramble in this book was chosen for its accessibility from one or more of the main tourist centres on Cyprus. Walks 1-7 are ideal for anyone staying in the **Troodos/Platres** area. Walks 8-9 are reachable too, but are set in mountainous country, remote from any major centres, and a considerable journey on rough roads is necessary to reach them, wherever you are based. From **Paphos**, take your choice of Walks 10-16, but consider 8, 9 and all walks on the Akamas Peninsula as well. From **Polis and Lachi**, Walks 17-23 are nearest, but 10-16 are easily reached by car. From **Limassol** Walks 24 and 25 are closest, but Walks 1-7 and 15 and 16 are worth considering. Walk 26 (Stavrovouni Monastery) is best approached from **Larnaca**, but is worth some kind of excursion from wherever you are staying. Walks 27 and 28 in the **Ayia Napa** region are also accessible from Larnaca.

I hope the book is set out so you can plan your walks easily. You might begin by considering the colour fold-out map between pages 16 and 17. Here you can see at a glance the overall terrain, the road network, and the exact location of the walking maps in the text. Flipping through

Goats on the Akamas uplands

the book, you will also find at least one photograph for each walk. Having selected a potential excursion from the map and the photographs, look over the planning information at the beginning of the walk. Here you'll find distance/hours, grade, equipment, and how to get there and return. Wherever feasible, I have also suggested a short version of the walk, for those lacking in time and/or ability.

When you are on the walk, you will find that the text begins with an introduction to the overall landscape and then quickly turns to a detailed description of the route itself. The **large-scale maps** (all 1:50,000) have been annotated to show key landmarks. Times are given for reaching certain points on the walk. Giving times is always tricky, because they depend on so many factors, but the times I give are rather slower than my own walking time. Note that they **do not include any stops**! Allow extra time for picnics, photography, and pottering about.

These symbols are used on the walking maps:

Symbol	Meaning	Symbol	Meaning
▬	main road	●→	water tank, spring, etc.
▬	secondary road (in white on the touring map)	📷/▲	best views/forest
═	track on the touring map	700	height (in metres)
——— - - -	other track, footpath	*P*	picnic spot (see pp14-18)
→	main walk and direction	✝/+	monastery, church/shrine
(12) →	alternative walk	🚌/🚗	bus stop/car parking
	windmill/lighthouse	⚒/∩	mine/cave
T/⛩	forest telephone/picnic tables		military area/firing range
			signpost/antenna or pylon

1 TROODOS • CHROMION • MOUNT OLYMPUS • TROODOS

See map pages 54-55; see also illustrations pages 2, 32, 51, 52 61

Distance: 15km/9.3mi; 4h (add 1h return for the summit detour)

Grade: quite easy; gentle ups and downs

Equipment: walking boots or stout shoes, sweater, sunhat, water, picnic; waterproof in winter

How to get there and return: 🚗 to/from Troodos. A hire car gives greatest flexibility, but a shared private taxi from and to Limassol is a reasonable option. A 🚐 minibus from Limassol to Platres operates in the high season; check times with the tourist office. If you travel by minibus, take a taxi from Platres to Troodos to start the walk, and arrange a return pickup at Troodos. Allow plenty of time to enjoy the day.

Shorter walk: Troodos to Chromion (9km/5.6mi; 2h30min; easy). Follow the main walk to Chromion and meet your taxi there.

Alternative walk: Artemis Trail (7km/4.3mi; 2h; quite easy). 🚗 to the start of the nature trail, some 0.4km up the road to the Olympus summit.

There is a riding stable at Troodos, so the description of 'one horse town' is not entirely accurate. But it nearly fits. Despite recent 'improvements', Troodos is neither a town nor a village, but a collection of shops, small hotels, cafés and souvenir stalls. Even the open-air kebab houses and their squabbling owners have given way to a new rest area. I miss them! Troodos is a community that springs to life in summer and at weekends and is the centre of activity during Cyprus's short ski season. Four kilometres from Troodos by road is the highest point on the island — Mount Olympus (1952m/6400ft), the focal point of this, one of my favourite walks in the Troodos region. Though romantically named, the 'top of Cyprus' serves a prosaic function as the site of a TV transmitter and radar installation — the latter featuring enormous 'golf balls' which are a distinctive landmark. One does not have to go right to the summit on this walk, but it would be a pity not to do so, having come this far.

The walk starts opposite the telephone exchange building at the northern end of Troodos' main (and only) street, at the wooden archway shown on page 52 (don't confuse it with a similar nearby departure point for the CTO pavilion). Much of the walk is along the Atalante Nature Trail established by the Forestry Department and the Cyprus Tourism Organisation. Grab a leaflet (if you're lucky) at the archway, and be educated as well as invigorated...

At about **8min** the path curves round the back of the Jubilee Hotel, much favoured by skiers and walkers. The trail doubles back on itself at the head of a small 'gulch', which is a dry as a bone most of the year. Keep left at a fork (the right option leads to the Artemis Trail... and is

The 'golf balls' of the radar installation and the mysterious, abandoned Berengaria Hotel are both distinctive features of the Olympus landscape.

also our return route). Soon you can look south towards Platres and beyond. At about **25min** a wide panorama opens up, with even Limassol's salt lake visible on a clear day.

At **45min** you reach a three-way signpost and an open area with picnic potential and striking views (Picnic 1). Ignore the sign and follow the path in front of a wooden bench. Near nature trail point No 25, observe a stream of drinking water on the right (but it may be dry during summer). Follow the trail past a viewpoint at No 31, and come at No 37 to the tunnel entrance to the Hadjipavlou chromium mine, which was worked from the 1950s until 1982. Keep out, if you have any sense! But you'll find shade here for a refreshment stop. Come soon to a signpost and follow the Chromion path.

At around **1h50min**, screech to a halt near trail point No 48, to observe to your left Prodhromos village and the distinctive, abandoned Berengaria Hotel. On the horizon you'll see Throni, the peak above Kykko Monastery where Archbishop Makarios is buried.

At **2h05min** the way becomes a little scree-like for a short distance. A few minutes later, notice a small abandoned quarry to the right; then, further on, look up the hillside for a clear view of the Mount Olympus TV mast.

Chromion, the end of the nature trail, comes up at around **2h30min**. Exit here the weary, the sun-struck and the tight of schedule. Onward to Olympus the rest of us! Ignore the road; look right and follow an indistinct track upwards through fallen pine cones until you very quickly reach a clear path (this is the Artemis Trail; see Alternative walk). Turn left and at **2h40min** see a ski-lift. The path zigzags to the right to gain a little height and in a few minutes offers some striking views across to the Turkish-occupied zone and west to the coast above Paphos.

At around **3h** you should reach the secondary road

leading to the summit. All those for the 'golf balls' turn right along the road and follow it for about 1.5 km/1mi, passing the Cyprus Ski Club café (only open in the skiing season), returning to this spot after viewing.

Cross the road to the Artemis Nature Trail archway and route indicator. Here you have another, slightly shorter (7km) circuit of Mount Olympus, not vastly different from the one just completed, but higher and a touch more dramatic. Save this for another day, *or* combine the two trails for a good long ramble.

For the main walk, start out along Artemis, but then take the broad track that heads off to the left between trail points No 4 and 5. Then, after about 450m/yds, go left on a rocky track; it curves back north to rejoin the Atalante Nature Trail between points 9 and 10. Turn left again, and you should be back at Troodos at **4h** or sooner, after a splendid introduction to Mount Olympus. There are spectacular views at any time of year, with richly coloured flora in spring, and you will have barely climbed a hill all day. But do take a jumper. Snow can lie here after Easter!

Troodos in snow — very pretty, but make sure you don't try to follow any of the trails if the powder is still deep!

2 TROODOS • MAKRYA KONTARKA • TROODOS

See map pages 54-55; see also photographs pages 2, 32, 50, 61

Distance: 6km/4mi; 1h45min

Grade: easy; also level walking

Equipment: stout shoes, sunhat, water, picnic; sweater and waterproof in winter

How to get there and return: as Walk 1, page 48

Alternative walk: Troodos — Makrya Kontarka — Caledonian Falls — Platres (12km/7.4mi; 3h40min; fairly easy descent of 600m/1970ft). At the crossroads reached in 40min, turn right and follow an easy, rough forestry road for about 5km to Kryos Potamos, where you can pick up Walk 3. See also Walk 5 for the mule trail route to Platres.

This is a splendid, easy stroll which packs a wide variety of scenery into a short distance. It's a lovely way of getting some Troodos air after a drive up from Limassol.

From the southern end of Troodos main street, follow the signpost to the Civic Restaurant. Pass the restaurant (on your left), then come to the police station on the right. Opposite is a wooden archway similar to that at the start of Walk 1. You may (or, more likely, may not) find a CTO

Benches some 8 minutes along the Persephone Trail (a shady setting for Picnic 2)

Nature trail archway at the start of Walk 1

nature trail leaflet in the dispenser. **Start out** on this, the Persephone Trail, and in about **8min** come to the particularly attractive stand of tall pine trees and cluster of benches shown on the preceding page (Picnic 2).

You don't need a rest yet, so keep going and at **15min** reach an obvious viewpoint. Look back the way you have come and enjoy a fine view of Mount Olympus — its old name is Khionistra. Then look ahead: to the left see the unmistakeable landmark of the Pano Amiandos asbestos mine, with the road to Kakopetria, Galata and Nicosia just to its left. Should you travel that road during your stay, you will get an entirely different view of Pano Amiandos from the other side. It is a mighty excavation!

Come at **40min** to a 'crossroads' (see Alternative walk and also Walk 5); keep ahead here, and at **50min** you will be enjoying a spectacular panorama. This point of the walk, an area known as Makrya Kontarka (Picnic 2), is some 1680m/5510ft above sea level and affords breathtaking views of Pano Amiandos, Trimiklini and Saittas villages, the peaks of Kionia and Kakomallis... not to mention Limassol harbour and salt lake, plus countless village vineyards. Plenty of seats are provided here, an ideal place to settle down with flask and sandwiches, or my idea of a good picnic — a stick of *soujoukko* and a nip of Cyprus brandy!

The best way back is the same path in reverse, but it provides further opportunity to enjoy the splendid views ... or you could turn left at the 'crossroads' and follow the Alternative walk or Walk 5 down to Platres.

3 TROODOS • CALEDONIAN FALLS • PLATRES

See map pages 54-55; see also photographs pages 2, 32, 50, 61

Distance: 4km/2.5mi; 1h35min

Grade: quite easy descent of about 450m/1475ft, but beware of turned ankles where the stony path twists and turns.

Equipment: stout shoes, sunhat, water, picnic; sweater and waterproof in winter

How to get there and return: as Walk 1, page 48. Take a taxi to Kryos Potamos or Troodos to start the walk.

Alternative walk: See Alternative walk 2, page 51.

The nature trail on which this walk is based is a mere 2km long — even shorter than Walk 2. But the going is somewhat harder because of twists and turns in the path and stepping stones which criss-cross the stream many times as you make your way to the Caledonian Falls.

The walk starts about 1.5km south of Troodos on the main road to Platres, opposite a sign indicating 'Kryos Potamos'. (You can also reach it after a pleasant 2km walk from Troodos, on a quiet, zigzagging secondary road that leads off the Platres road opposite the signpost to the Dolphin Restaurant.) Find the familiar CTO wooden archway, at which point stop and listen... for if it's high summer you may be hearing your first babbling brook of the holiday. Many streams dry up in summer, but not this one. At about **6min** look out on the right for the first of numerous stream crossings. At **15min** a series of wooden steps cut into the hillside achieves a descent of about 20m/65ft in a short distance. They are steep, so take extra care in wet weather.

Nimble walkers might reach the falls (Picnic 3) in **35min**. But those of us peering at all the points of interest on the nature trail — and the less fleet of foot — might take around **45min**.

Shortly after you leave the falls the nature trail ends, and a post indicates the way to Psilon Dhendron. Follow the track to another signpost, where the aroma of grilled trout should lead you round to the left. You reach the trout farm and restaurant at around **1h15min**. Cross the metalled road and continue into Platres (**1h35min**).

The Caledonian Falls (seen here in summer) are at their best in early spring when the Troodos snow melts (Picnic 3)

Kykko
Lefka
Kakopetria
PEDOULHAS
1500
Prodhromos
1600
T 1300
PRODHROMOS
1700
1800
1900
1
Palea Kh
OLYM
Paleomylos
T
1800
Kambi tou Kaloyerou
1700
1
T
6
1300
Ayios
Dhimitrios
Xerokolymbos
1200
1600
1100
1500
Argakin tous
Xerokolymbous
Atalante
Ayios
Yeoryios
1400
6
Trooditissa
T
6
Livadhoudhion
1200
1300
6
1100
1000
900
Ayii
Anargyri
800
900
T
PHINI
Elea (10km)
PLAT
Kato
Platres
Mandria, Omodhos

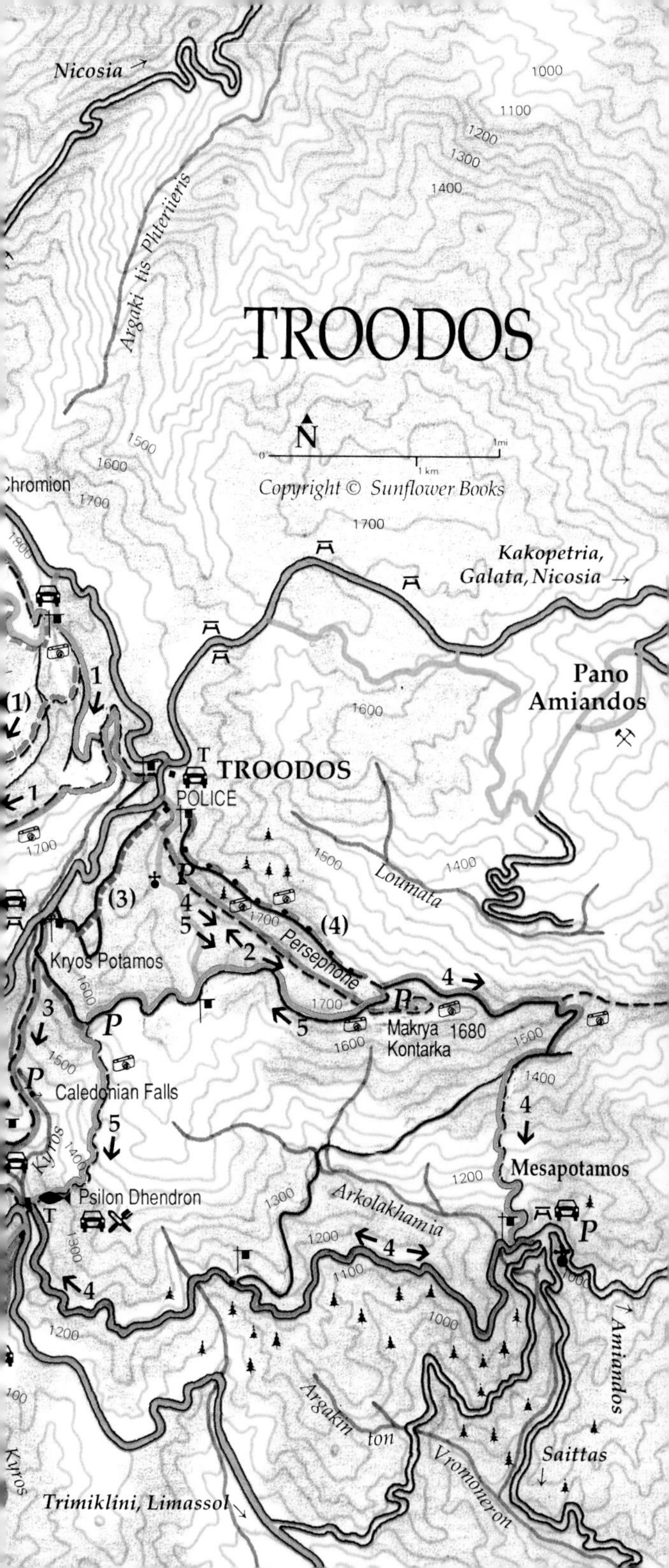

Nicosia →
Argaki tis Phterijeris
TROODOS
Copyright © Sunflower Books
Chromion
Kakopetria, Galata, Nicosia →
Pano Amiandos
TROODOS
POLICE
Loumata
Persephone
Kryos Potamos
Makrya Kontarka 1680
Caledonian Falls
Kyros
Mesapotamos
Psilon Dhendron
Arkolakhamia
Argakin ton Vromoneron
Amiandos
Saittas
Kyros
Trimiklini, Limassol

4 TROODOS • MAKRYA KONTARKA • MESAPOTAMOS MONASTERY • PLATRES

See map pages 54-55; see also photographs pages 2, 32, 50, 61

Distance: 16km/10mi; 4h

Grade: quite easy, but there is one steep section on a gravelly path. Tota descent: just over 800m/2600ft; ascent about 200m/650ft. The end o the walk can be a bit of a slog in hot weather.

Equipment: boots or stout shoes, sunhat, water, picnic; sweater an waterproof in winter

How to get there and return: As Walk 1, page 48. Take a taxi to Troodo to start.

Alternative walks: See Walks 2, 3 and 5.

Cyprus lace-makers

Mesapotamos Monastery (Picnic 4) is awaiting redevelopment. There is an 'official' picnic place with tables nearby.

Grand views await you on this easy-to-follow but longish ramble which takes in a vast opencast mine and a deserted monastery.

There are two ways of **starting the walk** at Troodos. The first is to take a road (a Cyprus road... it's really a track!) signposted 'Mesapotamos 13km' about 100m short of the police station at the southern end of the main street. I prefer to set off as if doing Walk 2 and enjoy the Persephone Nature Trail. At the **40min** 'crossroads' turn left and join the original road to Mesapotamos, which can be stony underfoot at times.

From here there are closer views of Pano Amiandos asbestos mine. Is it an eyesore or part of the landscape? Form your own judgment. At about **1h**, during which time the mine has dominated the view, it suddenly disappears from sight, as the track turns sharply right, twice. Those who have done Walk 2 will recognise, but be closer to, the vast panorama away to the left.

The track falls away sharply to the left for a short time, but after about 250m/yds, you can take a descending path to the left, on a gentler incline. Keep straight down this forest path (ignore any crossing paths or tracks). At first the descent is very steep (and sometimes slippery with rubble), but about halfway down an easier track comes underfoot. It takes you to a wider track, where a signpost indicates 'Platres 7km' to the right. You'll return to this signpost after visiting the old monastery, which is a short walk to the left and reached after about **2h** or so.

The monastery (Picnic 4) is in a wooded valley, helpfully cooler than the various tracks that lead to it, and you'll find there a welcoming stream of drinking water. But there are no other facilities: make sure you've brought a picnic! There is an official site nearby, if you like those sort of places. I'd rather find shade under a tree.

Return to the aforementioned signpost. The track rises some 200m over 4km. Beyond a signpost ('Platres 3km), it's a pleasant stroll to the trout farm and Platres itself, reached at about **4h**, depending on the heat and the feet.

5 TROODOS • MAKRYA KONTARKA • MULE TRAIL • PLATRES

See map pages 54-55; see also photographs pages 2, 32, 50, 61

Distance: 10km/6.2mi; 2h30min

Grade: quite easy; a descent of 600m/1965ft; slight risk of vertigo on the mule trail

Equipment: stout shoes, sunhat, water, picnic; sweater and waterproof in winter

How to get there and return: as Walk 1, page 48. Take a taxi to Troodos to start the walk.

Alternative walks: See Walks 2 and 3.

Here's another very appealing way to reach Platres from Troodos on foot... by mule trail. This ancient route provides some terrific views towards Limassol on the descent.

Begin by following Walk 2 along the Persephone Nature Trail, and turn off to the right at the **40min** 'cross-roads' (perhaps walk to the 50min viewpoint first, then return and turn left). Almost immediately you will have superb views to your left, and at about **45min** the track curves left under the radar 'golf balls' at Troodos.

In **1h** or less come to a T-junction and turn left at the sign to 'Kryos Potamos 3km' (see Alternative walk 2). After a minute or two observe a brown bench on the right and a very battered signpost on the left that long since forgot where it was pointing to! Follow it anyway, and at about **1h10min** look for a green bench on your left (Picnic 5). It's a nice spot to rest briefly and enjoy the views.

Just below the seat you pick up the old mule trail that leads all the way to Platres. It does a lot of zigzagging, crosses a bit of scree where vertigo is a slight risk, but offers magnificent views towards Limassol, and over Platres, your final destination.

About an hour below the seat you will come to a dirt road. Cross it diagonally and resume the trail, which zig-zags again. Follow the arrows and come to the trout farm at Psilon Dhendron (Walk 3). To the left is the road from Mesapotamos (followed at the end of Walk 4). From here stroll 1km into Platres in **2h30min**. Maybe less.

Cress (Arabis purpurea)

TROODITISSA

ee map pages 54-55; see also photographs pages 32 and 61

istance: 10km/6.2mi; 2h45min

rade: easy, with one uphill stretch of 2.5km (just over 150m/490ft)

quipment: walking boots or stout shoes, sunhat, water, picnic; sweater nd waterproof in winter

ow to get there and return: as Walk 1, page 48. To both start and end e walk, use a taxi from Platres to Trooditissa and be sure to arrange a turn pickup, allowing enough time to enjoy the walk.

horter walk: Trooditissa Monastery — Kambi tou Kaloyerou (5.5km/ .4mi; 1h30min; grade and access as above). Arrange with the Platres xi driver to collect you at the Kambi tou Kaloyerou picnic site on the rodhromos road — but you will not have escaped the climb!

Trooditissa Monastery, nestling in the Troodos Mountains some 5km northwest of Platres, was founded in 250AD, and among its treasures are ancient icons and a eather belt decorated with silver medallions. Tradition as it that wearing the belt promotes fertility in women. ntil quite recently, one of the monks would happily roduce this potent object for visitors, but perhaps beause of increasing tourism, the monastery is now closed the public. But that does not detract from the appeal of his most scenic walk.

The walk starts from a point about 50 metres beyond he monastery entrance, where a signpost indicates yios Dhimitrios 9km'. That is not our destination but it the track to follow. It soon curves round to the southest, offering magnificent views over Phini village in the alley far below. At **20min** reach another track leading ff to the right, but ignore it; you will recognise this unction on the way back — it's the return route. Continue own to the left, and in **25min** you'll see a signpost ndicating Phini 4km. Ignore this too!

At **50min** come to a clearing where there may be a gnpost indicating 3km walked. Ayios Dhimitrios is raight on, but we turn right, for a gentle climb of 2.5km the Kambi tou Kaloyerou picnic site on the Prodhromos oad. This section of the walk is not in the 'brutal' ategory, but it can be a bit of a sweat in hot weather. top for a breather occasionally and puzzle over the

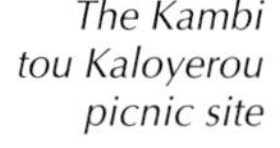

The Kambi tou Kaloyerou picnic site

View to Phini from the Trooditissa track. Phini has a local museum an a pottery of some note.

inviting-looking tracks that lead downhill, but ignore then all. Keep on uphill to the Trooditissa/Prodhromos roa (**1h30min**). The picnic site across the road is very obvious and a pleasant location, with tables and benches amon the tall trees. There is also an area set aside for barbecu cooking, and a play area for young children. This is a excellent place to take a break, or end the walk if yo have a pick-up arranged.

Leaving the picnic site, turn left along the road toward Trooditissa, and follow it for some 10 minutes, ignorin the first track you see off to the right. In about **1h40mi** you'll come to a sharp right turn in the road. Stop, an locate a track that leads off the road to the right, close t a pair of concrete water tanks. You now follow this trac all the way back to the junction first encountered 2 minutes from the start of the walk. In its early stages, thi track may show evidence of rockfalls; it is liberally strew with rocks and boulders. The risk of further falls is greate after heavy rain, and it's possible that you will have t return to the road and follow this to Trooditissa, shoul you be walking in winter or early spring.

The track is really a high-level version of the outwar journey and offers spectacular views to the south an west. At around **2h25min** reach the junction first passe 20min into the walk; turn left and in **2h45min** you shoul be back at Trooditissa, where a café opens in summer an on *some weekends* in winter.

MADHARI RIDGE

istance: 7.5km/4.7mi, 2h30min; optional extra 3.5km (1h) round
t Adelphi

rade: moderate climb of under 300m/980ft; some short, steep
retches

quipment: walking boots or stout shoes, sunhat, water, picnic; sweater
nd waterproof in winter

ow to get there and return: 🚗 by car, leave Troodos on the Nicosia
oad. Beyond Pano Amiandos, turn off right for Kyperounda. After about
km, turn left towards 'Spilia 5km'. Park at the nature trail arch on the
ght, 2.5km along.

Mt Adelphi is the second highest point on Cyprus (1613m/5290ft), and this walk to it along an exposed dge is even more spectacular than the approach to Mt Olympus. It can be strenuous for short stretches, and ne track stony, but the views are stunning — from the orthern, Turkish side of the island to the south, where yperounda clings to the opposite hillside like magic.

Start out at the nature trail arch: climb sharply to the ght and, when you come to a fork where you can go head or left, keep left. You soon reach a rocky outcrop vith a wonderful view northwards towards Morphou ay. At around **15min** come to a bench (Picnic 7) from vhere there are equally breathtaking views over yperounda and towards the Pano Amiandos mine and ne 'golf balls' on Mt Olympus.

Walk the trail through pine trees, and at around **40 min** rop down to a small clearing with views over the Aesaoria Plain and towards Mt Adelphi — another setting or Picnic 7. This could mark the end of a short version of his walk if you didn't fancy the climb ahead. But it isn't s bad as it looks, honestly! It can be quite cool and

ıdas trees in the Troodos foothills

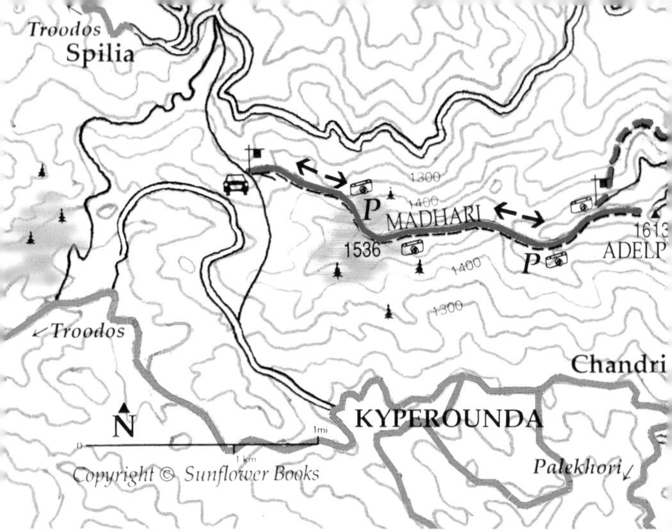

breezy on top, even in summer, so it's a good idea to pac a sweater, whatever the season.

Skip up to Madhari Ridge like a moufflon, and you'l be rewarded with wonderful views! You'll be up top a about **50min**. Turn left and walk along the ridge, takin the air, and lots of photographs. You'll see Kyperound again to your right, and Chandria with its striking moder church. Reservoirs glimmer between the two villages.

White cairns indicate viewpoints to your left (clim slightly to reach them), then Mt Adelphi with the fire watch point at its peak comes into view. Climb the las stretch for some truly magnificent views and, if you wish do the extra signposted circuit (add one hour).

Then retrace your steps to the nature trail arch (**2h 30min**). If you haven't been impressed by the views fron the ridge, the brandy sours are on me if we ever meet!

Kyperounda from Madhari Ridge (Picnic 7)

꞉ STAVROS TIS PSOKAS

istance: 11km/6.8mi; 3h35min

rade: moderate, with ascents of bout 400m/1300ft

quipment: stout shoes or walk-g boots, sunhat, water, picnic; weater and waterproof in winter

low to get there and return: 🚗 y car from Paphos via Kanna-iou; from Polis via Lyso; from roodos via Kykko Monastery. *IB: In winter and early spring, ccess may not be possible.* Park ıst over 1km out of Stavros on ıe ascending road to Kykko, as close as possible to the Horteri Nature rail wooden arch on the right. Or park at Stavros (add 2.5km).

hort walks

Horteri Nature Trail (5km/3mi, 2h15min; ascent 200m/650ft). ollow the main walk to the 1h50min-point, then head left downhill to our starting point (follow 'Stavros 3km').

Moutti tou Stavrou Nature Trail (2.5km/1.6mi; 45min; easy). Park km north of Stavros, by the nature trail sign, at the junction for Livadhi, 'roisha and Kykko. Climb steps up to the nature trail and pick up the ıain walk just after the 1h50min-point. When you return to the bench t the fork, descend to your car.

t is a venturesome traveller indeed who makes an excursion into one of the island's most attractive but solated regions. Roads in these parts can be little more han rough tracks, but passable in standard autos *in dry veather.* The rewards are enormous, the scenery verdant, nd there's an off-chance of seeing the rare Cyprus sheep – the moufflon — which was once almost extinct. But it s a very shy creature!

The Forestry Department runs a forest station at Stavros vhere there's a small café, and hostel accommodation see pages 40-41). To encourage intimate acquaintance vith the environment, the department has also created wo walks around Stavros, and information about the area s available from the forestry office.

The walk begins at the Horteri Trail archway. The trail keep left at a fork a short way from the start) zigzags ortheast uphill, with excellent views over the whole alley setting of Stavros. In about **45min** come to a green eat near a junction with a track. Turn left and climb quite teeply, heading for a peak with a fire-watch point. The vay curves right, then left, before reaching a junction vith a wider track (**1h**). Follow this track to the right, oming at **1h15min** or less to another wooden nature trail ırch, by the side of the 'main road' from Stavros to Kykko.

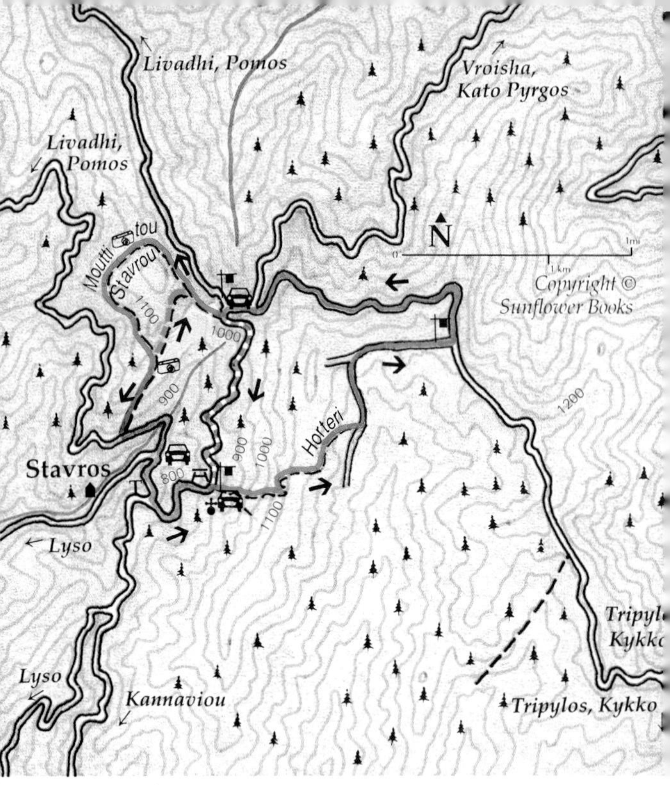

Turn left, and follow the road for about 2.5km, to a junction of tracks (**1h50min**), all of them clearly signposted. Short walk 1 heads left here, following 'Stavros'.

The main walk now explores the Moutti tou Stavrou footpath, which begins here at another wooden arch. Ascend the trail to a fork and keep right (Short walk 2 will return to this point after completing a loop). Soon, from a plateau, there is a fine view reaching west to the Akamas Peninsula. Later, a lovely stretch along a north/south ridge affords more magnificent views. You will come to a sign indicating that reafforestation is in progress on the opposite hillside (see photograph caption opposite). Here Short walk 2 heads left to complete the circuit. The main walk turns right, zigzagging southwest down the ridge. The surface underfoot is rather loose with rubble, so take care. The views all around are superb, and you should spot a seat at which a sign proclaims 'nice view of the Stavros valley'... with which there can be no argument.

The trail descends to a track (**2h50min**), where you turn left to Stavros (**3h05min**). From here walk up the Kykko road back to your car at the Horteri Trail arch (**3h35min**).

9 CEDAR VALLEY AND MT TRIPYLOS

Distance: 14km/8.7mi, 4h

Grade: quite easy, with an ascent of about 250m/820ft

Equipment: walking boots or stout shoes, sunhat, water, picnic; sweater and waterproof in winter

How to get there and return: 🚗 by car from Paphos via Kannaviou and Stavros; from Troodos via Kykko Monastery. *NB: In winter and early spring, access may not be possible via Stavros.* Park at the Dhodheka Anemi junction (8km from Stavros on the Kykko road).

Short walk: Mt Tripylos (4km/2.5mi; 1h15min; grade as above). At the junction you will see a gated track (from which vehicles are now barred) signposted to Mt Tripylos. Park here and simply follow the track uphill for 2km and return the same way.

Whether you make this walk your prime target for the day, or choose the shorter version while on a trip to Kykko, you are sure to enjoy it! The views are splendid, and the surroundings beautiful.

The longer (main) walk is easy to follow, largely on shaded Cyprus earthen roads among fragrant pines and towering cedars. **Begin at** the Dhodheka Anemi junction: follow the road signposted 'Cedar Valley 10km'. It *is* technically a road (non-metalled), but in reality it makes a beautiful, easy-surfaced walk, gently downwards at this stage, through open pine woods.

You will pass three roads that head off to the right, and will experience stunning views to the south and west as your way curves gradually round to the east. After about **2h**, cedars will appear among the pine trees and become much more evident as you reach the area that gave rise to the name of Cedar Valley. You will come to a small

The forests around Stavros and Cedar Valley are in a healthier state now than they were early this century, and Winston Churchill can be credited for improving matters after 1907 when, as Under Secretary of State for the Colonies, he allocated funds for extensive tree-planting. The forests flourished in the ensuing years, but their welfare was not aided by the invading Turkish forces: in 1974 their air force needlessly set fire to over 150 square kilometres of trees. Recovery is continuing, thanks to the work of the Forestry Department. Please don't light fires, except at official sites!

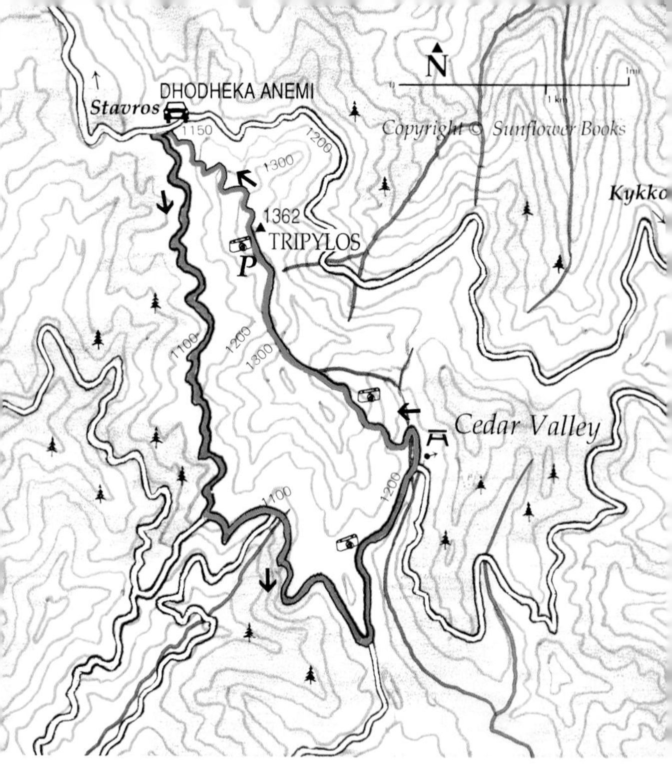

picnic area with a water supply, close to a group of plane trees (**2h30min**).

The route now leaves the forest road, and gently climbs the slopes of Mt Tripylos for 2.5km, with views opening out all around. If you are to see moufflon in the wild on your trip to Cyprus, this could be the day! Cedar trees are still very much in evidence as you approach the summit (**3h30min**). From this peak (1362m/4470ft) there are magnificent views — eastward to Troodos, westward to the Akamas, and north to Morphou Bay. At the top you'll see a fire-watch station and a small picnic area which couldn't have a more lovely setting (Picnic 9)!

From here it's a simple stroll of 2km back to Dhodheka Anemi and your car, reached in around **4h**. On a clear day the air could not have been fresher, nor the views more appealing.

10 AYIOS NEOPHYTOS

Distance: 8km/5mi, 2h

Grade: moderate, with a steep ascent near the start, a steep descent near the end, and some overgrown paths. Total ascent about 250m/820ft

Equipment: walking boots or stout shoes, sunhat, water, long trousers

How to get there and return: car or taxi to/from Ayios Neophytos

The 12th-century monastery of St Neophytos is about 10km north of Paphos and dedicated to a man who was a noted scholar and writer, devoted man of God, and a hermit who chose a life of reclusion in caves that can still be seen by visitors. Some have beautiful frescoes that can be closely inspected, whether on a car outing or as a prelude to this circuit of the monastery valley.

Start out from the monastery by walking back towards Paphos, past the turning for Tala. After about 650m/yds, look out for an old stone warehouse with recent extension, and 50m/yds before it, turn sharp left on a farm track. This climbs steeply through vineyards, but the effort is rewarded with ever-improving views over the monastery.

After about 350m/yds the track merges with another, and you keep ahead, bearing left. You touch briefly on a metalled road, then head left on a track below the summit of Melissovounos. Continue gently uphill towards the radio aerials. It's worth a detour of 300m/yds to the top, to gain views towards Paphos and the coast. Be here at about **45min**.

Go back to the main path and turn right to follow it along the crest of a hill, gently undulating, and surrounded by vineyards. You come to a quiet metalled road (**1h**), where you turn left towards the village of Kili. After about 1km you will pass two signs to Kili (opposite the second sign there is a bus shelter). A few metres/yards beyond this second sign, turn left on a road. This leads

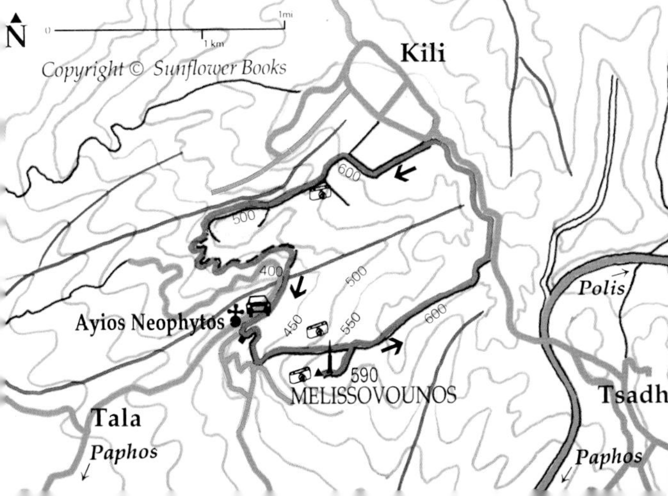

Wall painting at Ayios Neophytos; below: the monastery courtyard

past an isolated house on the left, bears right, and ends after a few hundred metres/yards. Turn left downhill through vineyards, enjoying splendid views towards the distant coast. At a junction, keep straight on, then bear slightly left downhill. After 200m/yds turn right at a fork, and inspect the gorge over to your right.

The way bends left towards Melissovounos, but very soon afterwards take a steep path descending to the right. Then, after about 25m/yds, look out on the left for a narrow, indistinct, stony path. This is rather overgrown with thorny bushes, but after 300m/yds you will get views of Ayios Neophytos. At about **2h** you will be back at your starting point.

11 KISSONERGA TO CORAL BAY

IMPORTANT: This walk is no longer possible as described below; see STOP PRESS on page 124.

Distance: 8.5km/5.3mi, 2h30min **Grade**: easy, ascents 100m/330ft

Equipment: stout shoes, sunhat, water, picnic, swimming things

How to get there: car or taxi to Kissonerga; by car park near the sports ground near the church. Or from Paphos (not in the timetables; check at the tourist office or with the ALEPA Bus Co: see Timetable E7). *To return:* from Coral Bay to Paphos (Timetable E7), or to the junction of the Coral Bay/Kissonerga road, from where it is a 15min walk back to your car. Some buses return from Coral Bay to Paphos via Kissonerga (check at the tourist office or with the ALEPA Bus Co: see Timetable E7).

In recent years this very popular ramble to the main irrigation reservoir of the Paphos region has been closed by the military. ***It is no longer possible to do the walk as described below,*** but a 'Landscaper' who winters on Cyprus has sent an alternative version: *see page 124.*

The walk starts at Kissonerga, a village which straddles the Paphos/Coral Bay road. Cross the sports pitch beside the church, then cross the main road. Head up a surfaced track ('Apis Street'); you pass the village cemetery, on your left, after less than 100m/yds. At **15min** join another track, turning left at a T-junction.You are now heading almost due north, walking past fruit and vegetable plots.

At around **35min** come to a definite junction; ahead you will see a large military camp built into the hillside, with accompanying signs forbidding all photography. Turn right and, almost immediately, loop back left, to reach an open area outside the perimeter fence. Ahead

Coral Bay is a popular, but not overcrowded beach north of Paphos. It is named for the tiny fragments of pinkish-grey coral that form the shore.

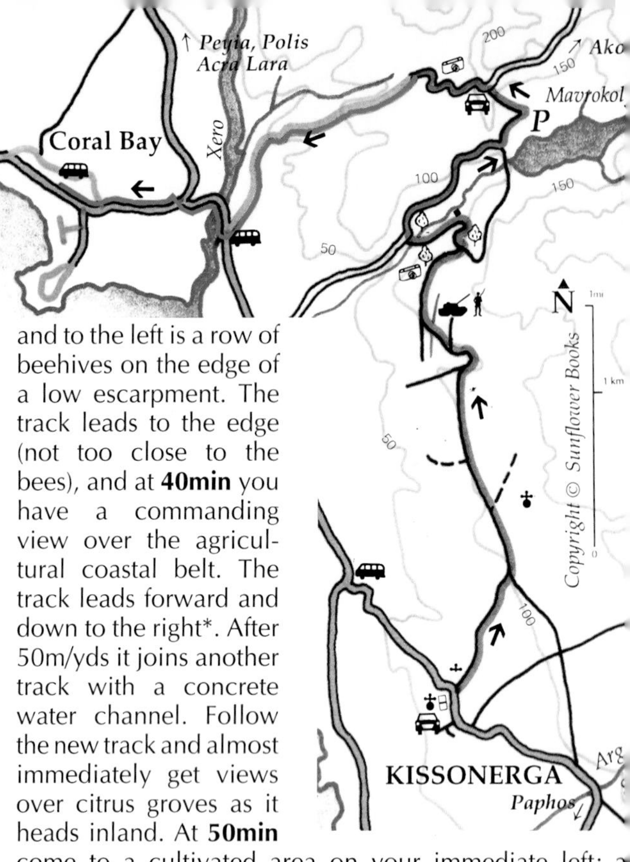

and to the left is a row of beehives on the edge of a low escarpment. The track leads to the edge (not too close to the bees), and at **40min** you have a commanding view over the agricultural coastal belt. The track leads forward and down to the right*. After 50m/yds it joins another track with a concrete water channel. Follow the new track and almost immediately get views over citrus groves as it heads inland. At **50min** come to a cultivated area on your immediate left; a minute or two later (after the track bends to the right), the way ahead is blocked by fencing and a metal gate.

Head off left alongside the fencing and zigzag down to the bottom of the valley, where a ruined building is opposite. Turn left through the citrus trees, away from the dam. After 300m/yds join a rough road and turn right uphill, climbing gently to the Mavrokolymbos Dam (Picnic 11; **1h15min**). Have a look at the steps, the sluice, a ruined building and an old bridge. A fine excuse for a breather!

Follow the track past the dam wall, and almost certainly see sheep and goats near the water's edge. About 500m/yds beyond the dam wall, at **1h20min**, turn sharp left on a track and climb to the Akoursos road (**1h35min**). Turn left: it's downhill almost all the way (4km) to Coral Bay (**2h30min**), where you can take a dip. Or flag down a bus as soon as you reach the busy coast road.

*If this track is blocked, follow the perimeter fence on the right, but leave the track to descend a footpath between two metal posts. *As soon as you reach the first row of trees in the valley,* head left along a drainage ditch, to pick up the track with the concrete water channel.

12 VINEYARDS OF KATHIKAS AND AKOURSOS

ee photograph page 25 **Distance**: 10km/6.2mi; 3h

;rade: easy, but with a stiff climb (280m/920ft) back out of Akoursos

quipment: walking boots or stout shoes, sunhat, water, picnic

low to get there and return: car to/from Kathikas

The Laona Project is a laudable attempt to breathe economic life back into some of the old villages of vestern Cyprus, while retaining their cultural and social dentity. Kathikas is home to the Laona Project Visitor Centre, where you'll find all the information you need, as vell as local produce and crafts for sale, and one of the best traditional tavernas in the area. This introductory .aona walk is taken (with consent) from an excellent booklet, *Discover Laona,* available at the Centre.

Begin at the Centre: turn right and walk south out of the village on a dirt road. Keep right at a fork (1.5km), and go straight on at a crossroads with a sign, 'Akoursos 4km'. You will see wild orchids by the wayside in spring.

After about 3.5km (**50min**), look out for a track joining rom the right (west) and remember it for your return. mmediately ahead is a lonely tree and an impressive view over the surrounding countryside. Soon you have views over Akoursos, a very old community set in a limestone valley. In the cliff opposite you'll see a distinctive cave, and at about **1h** observe a cave immediately to your ight, now used as a sheepfold.

At **1h20min** you should have reached the bottom of he valley and be exploring Akoursos, home to a disused nosque, an old olive press, a spooky cemetery — and some of the noisiest donkeys and dogs on Cyprus! Enjoy he place and read its history in *Discover Laona,* then brace yourself for the climb out. A sexy squiggle on a map often means a very unsexy gradient... so wheeze and splutter your way past the cave again, up to the aforementioned junction near he lonesome tree, and turn left.

This level track comes quickly to a T-junction: turn right. After 300m/yds, keep left at a fork. The pleasant return to Kathikas (**3h**) takes you through gentle vineyard scenery, past the tiny (but not very ancient) church of Ayia Marina.

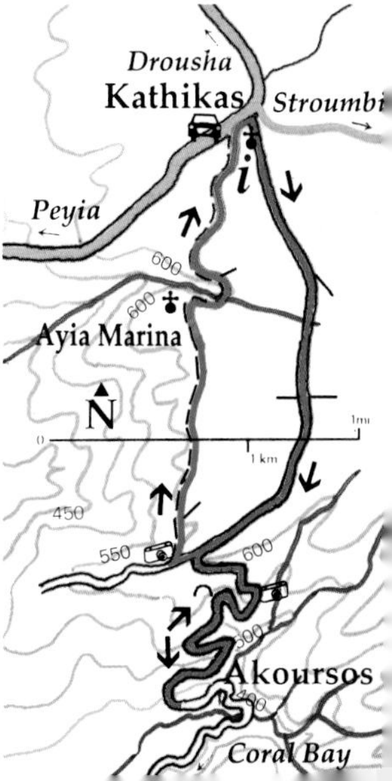

13 LARA BEACH

See map pages 98-99; see also photograph page 97

Distance: 3km/2mi; 1h

Grade: easy

Equipment: stout shoes, sunhat, water, picnic, swimming things

How to get there and return: car to/from Lara Beach, 27km north of Paphos via Coral Bay or from Paphos

Special note: *Access may be restricted in July-August during the nesting season of the rare green turtle. Please observe relevant warning signs.*

This attractive, unspoiled beach. setting for Picnic 13, can only be reached by car, or perhaps on a sea cruise out of Paphos during summer (check at the tourist office for times). By car it is a leisurely drive north through Kissonerga passing close to Coral Bay, then Ayios Yeoryios. (A short detour here will show you ar attractive fishing refuge and interesting church over looking the sea.)

The whole area dates back to Roman times and ha been the scene of much excavation. Thus far the road i metalled, but now you face a 6km drive on a very rougl track. You'll make it, but check your dental filling regularly! After heavy rain the way could be very messy

Just beyond Ayios Yeoryios you'll see the signposte track to the Avagas Gorge on the right (Walk 14).

Thankfully, Lara has been spared the ravages of com merce, but one can tolerate and even give thanks for the single, seasonal taverna near the beach which caters fo most of Lara's visitors.

Apart from the taverna, there's absolutely nothing a Lara except wonderful coastal scenery and a quiet atmos phere. A most agreeable stroll can be made along anc around the beach for an hour or two.

Park and **start out** near the taverna, dropping down tc the shoreline. At the north end of the beach is a headlanc crossed by tracks, offering very pleasing views soutl along the coast and inland to the hills north of Peyia Close to Lara are the summer nesting grounds of the rare and protected green turtle.

North of Lara, the rough road gets even rougher before

petering out after a few kilometres (see 4WD options for Car tour 1 on page 24), but there are some very secluded coves along here if you fancy skinny-dipping.

Thankfully, the Akamas Peninsula which includes the Lara region was made a national park area early in the 1990s, thus ensuring its continued existence as a totally unspoiled, totally beautiful landscape.

14 AVAGAS GORGE

See map pages 98-99

Distance: 3km/2mi, 1h

Grade: quite easy, with some scrambling over boulders

Equipment: boots or stout shoes, sunhat, water, picnic

How to get there and return: 🚗 via Coral Bay and Ayios Yeoryios, 23km north of Paphos; see approach on page 72, first paragraph of the text.

From being almost a secret some years ago, the Avagas Gorge is now well visited, but it remains a dramatic geographical feature which deserves some respect. By far the best way to enjoy the whole gorge is on a guided trek with an organisation like ExAlt of Paphos whose leaders

In the depths of the gorge

know the region intimately and will take you into the gorge from the top... a difficult and potentially dangerous exercise without such help.

But it is easy enough to venture into the gorge from its mouth, walking only as far in as you feel comfortable. I suggest a foray of a mere 1km each way — this will let you see how its walls close in high above you and shut out much of the sunlight.

Drive to the turn-off above Ayios Yeoryios as described on page 72, and turn right. You will soon see the Viklari Taverna up on the left (call here on the way back and say hello to Savvas and his gorgeous great danes!). Drive down a track below and to the right of it. This drops down to a small parking place, where the track forks. **Start here** and walk through a gate to the left for 1km into the gorge... then back out again when you've had enough.

If you get as far as thick undergrowth, be aware that snakes (see Walking: Nuisances) are not unknown here in very hot weather. You may observe that some of the large boulders that you scramble round look newer than others... these came tumbling down the gorge walls in the most recent earthquake. Have a nice day!

Seen on a walk in the Akamas — perils of not wearing a sunhat?

Above: Sacred bones at Pano Arkhimandrita (see Walk 15)
Below: Unusual sights always catch my eye. This 3m-high upright stone near Pakhna is pierced with a hole. A mystery. But one old Cyprus legend suggested that if a man could not crawl through such a gap, he had cuckold's horns!

15 KHAPOTAMI GORGE

See also photographs page 27 and drawing page 75

Distance: 9.5km/6mi; 2h45min

Grade: moderate, with ascents of about 150m/500ft

Equipment: walking boots or stout shoes, sunhat, water, picnic

How to get there: 🚗 taxi from Paphos to Pano Arkhimandrita, shared to spread cost. It's a more expensive taxi journey from Limassol.
To return: 🚗 pre-arranged taxi from Alekhtora, or take the village taxi to the main road at Pissouri, from where you could telephone for a service taxi bound for Paphos or Limassol.

Circular walk for motorists: Kato Arkhimandrita — Khapotami Gorge — Kato Arkhimandrita (7.5km/4.7mi; 2h15min; grade as main walk). 🚗 car to Pano Arkhimandrita. After viewing the shrine, drive 2.5km on the rough road leading from the village water tanks, to park at Kato Arkhimandrita. Pick up the main walk at the 45min-point and follow it to just past the 2h15min-point, then take the track off left, over the hilltop, back to Kato Arkhimandrita and your car.

Alternative walk: Pano Arkhimandrita — Alekhtora — Petra tou Romiou (21km/13mi; 5h30min-6h; moderate-strenuous; access as main walk; return as Walk 16). Anyone with enough wind is strongly recommended to combine this walk with Walk 16 for an incredibly varied day.

Pano Arkhimandrita is situated among vineyards perched on hillsides, and the effect of the scenery when you first arrive is quite breathtaking. There is more to come.

Clearly signed in the village is a path which leads up past a taverna, then down some steps to the hermitage of Ayii Pateres, a tiny shrine nestling in a rock crevice. Herein is preserved a quantity of human bones. It is said they are of 318 saints who arrived on the coast at Pissouri in days of yore after fleeing persecution in Syria, only to meet an untimely death at the hands of local heathens. Your welcome in Arkhimandrita will be warmer, especially in either of the two coffee shops where locals will happily talk about their tiny community.

Visit the shrine (see drawing on page 75), respecting the 'don't touch' appeal, then **begin the walk** by zigzagging down the hillside to the right of the shrine. The path soon reaches a broader track (leading from the village

Arkhimandrita's green valley

church), where you should turn left. Some **25min** after leaving the shrine, having walked downhill with vineyards all around you, come to the valley floor and look through trees and bushes for a ruined mill on the left. It is almost overgrown. Look round to the right and locate an old bridge. Now retrace your steps a short way, and turn left on an obvious jeep track which leads through pine trees (above a parallel track where there are many beehives) to reach the abandoned village of Kato (Lower) Arkhimandrita at about **45min**. Walk through it and come at **50min** to a streambed and a junction.

Here you have two options. Cross the streambed and turn right on a *level* track, or, more interestingly, set out on a meandering path that starts *this side* of the streambed in the same direction, and criss-crosses the stream several times before merging with the level route at about **1h 05min** (**1h** on the level track).

From this point you are heading into the spectacular Khapotami Gorge and for the next hour you may feel vulnerable at times. This is quite wild country and is best experienced in a group, for safety's sake. Towering cliffs, birds of prey wheeling overhead, an infinite variety of trees and plants, lizards scampering at your feet... the holiday beaches seem a long way from this kind of Cyprus.

At around **1h35min** the path becomes a track and starts climbing to the left, and you will get steadily more

impressive views down into the impassable part of the gorge as you climb a series of zigzags for about 2km.

At maybe **2h15min** the track levels out and vineyards come into sight. Walk through two gates, taking care to close them behind you. For the Circular walk, look out for a track that leads off left shortly after the second gate. This climbs to a hilltop, then descends to the streambed at Kato Arkhimandrita, from where you can walk back to your car.

If you're doing the main walk and finishing at Alekhtora, simply follow the track ahead into the village (**2h45min**). If progressing to Walk 16 immediately (I hope you are!), stop short of Alekhtora and double back to the right on a track that skirts the vineyards and leads to a disused fruit-packing shed just south of the village. Turn right, and walk along the road for maybe 1km to a fruit-packing factory. *Now* turn to Walk 16, and set off for the famed Rocks of Aphrodite!

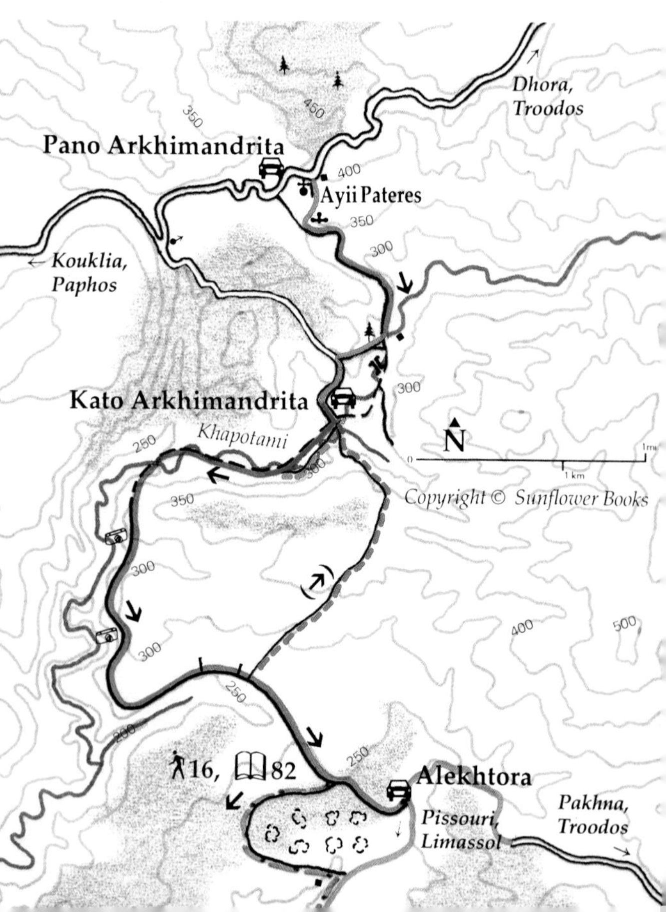

16 ALEKHTORA TO PETRA TOU ROMIOU (APHRODITE'S ROCKS)

See also photograph page 16
Distance: 11.5km/7mi; 3h15min
Grade: moderate, with a short rocky climb at the start (125m/400ft) and steep downhill scramble of 100m/330ft near the finish.
Equipment: walking boots or stout shoes, sunhat, water, picnic
How to get there: or service taxi to Pissouri (not in the timetables; check times with tourist office); then local taxi from Pissouri to Alekhtora
To return: service taxi from Petra tou Romiou. There is no public telephone at the tourist pavilion at Petra tou Romiou, so ask politely, and they will make the call for you.
Circular walk for motorists: Alekhtora — Khapotami overview — Alekhtora (6km/3.7mi; 2h; access/return by ; quite easy, with a climb/descent of about 125m/400ft). Park at the junction described in paragraph 2 below. Follow the main walk to the ruined farmhouse (1h 15min), then return to your car via the cobbled road.
Alternative walk: See Alternative walk 15, page 76.

A visit to Cyprus would not be complete without a trip to Aphrodite's Rocks — the birthplace of the Greek goddess of love. But why travel the easy way and miss all the fun? Come with me and visit a church with no windows, contemplate a mystery, and pretend to be a goat as you skip happily down a precipitous hillside!

Ask your taxi driver to drop you 1.5km south of Alekhtora, where the road makes a near-90-degree right turn, next to a small fruit-packing depot (see map on page 82). There is a sign here indicating Alekhtora. (This is also where you should park for the Circular walk.) At this junction, a rough road (really a track) heads northwest through vineyards. **Start out** along the track and zigzag uphill for about 1.5km. A good excuse for a breather at the top is the view over the countryside you have just traversed.

Having reached this height at around **25min**, turn right and follow a track past a solar-powered antenna unit. (As you can see on the map on page 82, we're heading for an overview of the Khapotami Gorge, the setting for Walk 15. Those of you who have just been in it might like to skip this detour: if so, do *not* fork right past the solar-powered antenna; keep ahead on the cobbled track, to walk directly to an old farmhouse... about which I shall have more to say on the following pages.)

Having passed the antenna on the track, turn diagonally left across open grassland after a short distance, walking through carob trees and bushes. This is very pleasant strolling — good bird-watching country — and you may catch sight of a distinctive blue 'roller'.

In about **40min** you'll come to the Khapotami overview which can be enjoyed at several points (Picnic 16) Come back from the overview and continue in a loopin direction to a goat enclosure on a hillside. There ar several tracks in this area, but you simply head for th goats (**1h**)! From the far side of the enclosure there ar more spectacular views over the gorge.

Now head back southeast from the enclosure (again i a looping direction) and aim for a pleasant stand of pin trees to the right. Walk through the trees, but stay near th eastern edge of them. After a few minutes, look out o your left for an old wall. Descend through a gap in th wall and come to a level grassy area. Cross this and yo will reach a church (**1h20min**) with white walls, a blu roof, and no windows.

Immediately beyond the church is the ruin of an 18th century 'khan' or coaching station: look out for an ol well near a broad track, which perhaps gave rise to thi area's name of Lakko tou Frankou (Well of the French).

Now look across the broad track (which is the partly cobbled road first seen at the 25min-point in the walk and observe a large, ruined farmhouse (**1h25min**) with threshing machine rusting quietly away to the rear. I'n not one for gossip, but if you want a whisper of scandal..

This goat enclosure is on the old road behind Petra tou Romiou, but it could be almost anywhere in the island's interior.

ɿe house was built a century ago, but an 'affair of the eart' led to a murder and it has not been occupied since. o the rear and to the right of the farmhouse, follow a ɔugh track. When it forks, keep right and start climbing radually. You will come to a viewpoint over a wide alley, with Pissouri away to the southeast.

Pause and think for a moment here, for the way ahead ets interesting. The next two or three kilometres are more question of the *right direction* than of looking for the ght path. You will see trails of sorts all over the place, ıostly made by goats!

From the viewpoint, head slightly downwards, keep-ıg to the right through a wooded area. *It is important not ɔ head too far southeast into the valley. You need to keep eight and stay to the right.* Just keep going forward, *due outh*, with the utmost confidence, and you will come at round **2h25min** to Laoni Ridge. From here there is a pectacular panorama towards the coast. Look at the eep slope in front of you and the goat enclosure below ı the distance, then figure out how to get there!

In wet weather the slope would be messy, but when ry, as it is most of the year, it is a comparatively easy cramble. Just like lining up a golf shot, work our your

best line. I find that a dog-leg, or goat-leg to the right i the best way. Take care and you will zigzag down th hillside quite neatly and be really proud of yourself at th bottom! Head for the goat enclosure and walk round i on a track which leads at **2h40min** to a crumblin metalled road (little more than a track). Turn right and se Petra tou Romiou in the distance.

Between you and Aphrodite's birthplace is a mer meandering descent. Plus a few hundred more goats. Th sea breezes around the tourist pavilion (**3h15min**) coul not be more welcome!

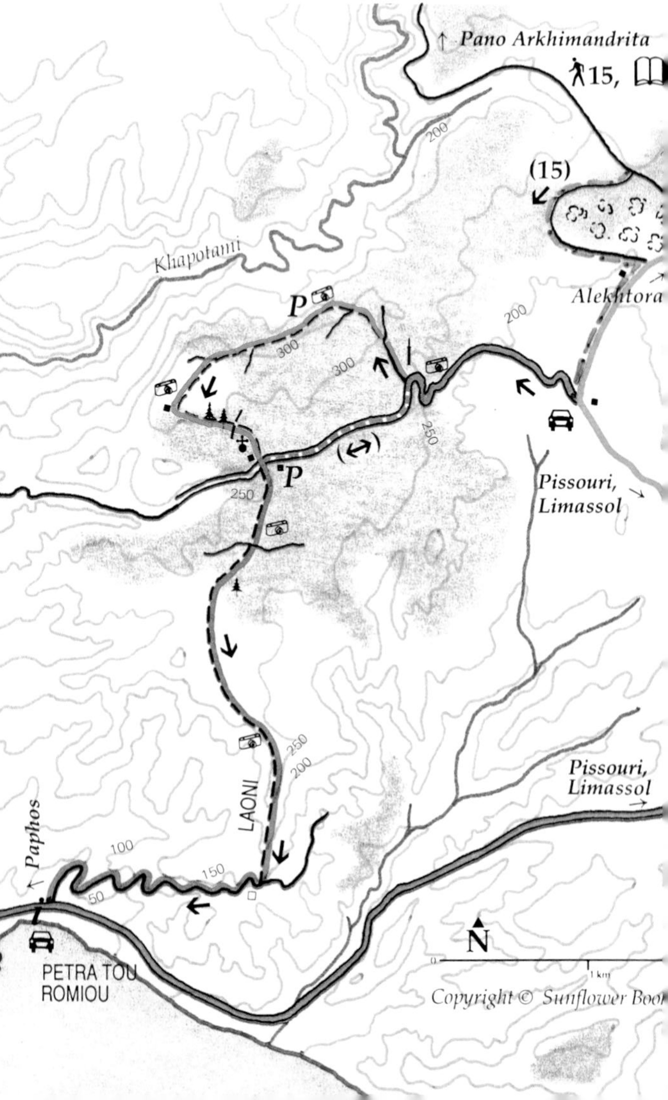

7 FONTANA AMOROSA COASTAL PATH

ee map on reverse of touring map; see also photograph page 87

istance: 6km/3.7mi, 1h45min

rade: quite easy, almost level walking

uipment: stout shoes, sunhat, water, picnic, swimming things

ow to get there and return: car to/from Lachi and from Lachi Fontana Amorosa; taxi from the Baths of Aphrodite back to Lachi

A wonderful walk with amazing views around the compass. Birdsong, butterflies, tiny lizards avoiding our feet, and a backdrop of mountains. What more could ne ask for? This walk takes you through unspoiled yprus, and long may it remain so.

The best approach to Fontana Amorosa is from the sea, o head initially for Lachi, where a boat can be hired to ke you there (ask at the Lachi Water Sports Centre). haring the boat journey with others will ensure that the ost is very reasonable. There is no proper landing area; he boatman will ask you to leap ashore on a hot and ocky outcrop which, at first sight, hardly merits its name. n reality the 'fountain of love' is a 5-metre deep well vhich you may not even find), but it doesn't matter! You ave only come for the pleasure of walking back to the aths of Aphrodite. For a longer ramble, it is interesting o walk to the very western tip of the island Cape Arnauti, n extra 3km/2mi return), passing the wrecked freighter gnello on the way.

The path from Fontana Amorosa **starts out** in an area f scrub. It may take a minute to locate, but once found, here is no problem. Simply head back eastwards and njoy the environment. The route wanders through scrub n both sides, but in **10min** you should be enjoying good iews of the sea. In **20min** come to a large warning sign bout military exercises and take good otice: don't touch anything suspicious-ooking. Equally, don't be deterred by the ed flag' aspect of this walk. It really is pectacular, with no evidence of the ilitary, except for the signs.

At **40min** the path turns inland for no ore than 50m/yds to avoid a gully, then it ains height as it continues eastwards. At bout **45min** you may catch sight of a cairn n a rock to the right, and of a particularly ttractive cove down left. At **1h10min** the ath climbs more steeply, but not for long, nd the views from this level are the finest

Plants of the Akamas scrub: strawberry tree (Arbutus unedo) *left; roc rose* (Cistus parviflorus) *right. Below: A delightfully secluded cove, see from above the Baths of Aphrodite*

of the walk. At the end of this stretch, one gets a panc ramic view over the Baths of Aphrodite, which should b reached in about **1h45min**. For this last descent, keep t the broader track on the right, not the narrower pat through low-lying trees... lest you disturb the goats.

At the baths ('Loutra Aphroditis' on the map) you hav two options. Your best bet for a return to Lachi is a tax — summoned on arrival, or pre-arranged. You *could* wal to Lachi along shingle beaches and the edges of fields but the way is unclear, the going frustrating, and the land scape indifferent compared with what has gone before.

8 THE 'APHRODONIS' TRAIL

ee map on reverse of touring map; see also photographs opposite

istance: about 7.5km/4.7mi; 2h, whichever trail you choose

rade: quite easy, but with a steep climb of 250m/820ft at the start. The phrodite Trail climbs an additional 100m/330ft. Both trails involve izgag descents on fairly loose rubble in places.

quipment: stout shoes (*not* sandals or trainers), sunhat, water, picnic

ow to get there and return: car or taxi to/from the Baths of phrodite tourist pavilion ('Loutra Aphroditis' on the map)

Walkers who have trod the Fontana Amorosa coastal path (Walk 17) know how special the views are in his 'top left-hand corner' of Cyprus. Imagine how much nore exciting those views are from 300 metres (1000 feet) igher up! Thanks to a pair of Forestry Department nature rails ('Aphrodite' and 'Adonis'), you can enjoy these iews and at the same time learn more about the flora and auna of the Akamas. A booklet fully explaining points of nterest is available from tourist offices, or from the orestry Department office near the Baths of Aphrodite ourist pavilion.

The high point of the walk along the Aphrodite Trail, in both senses, is reached after some 1h20min; from here ou look out westwards over Cape Arnauti.

The two trails share a common ascent (Picnic 18) at the start, lasting about an hour. The Aphrodite Trail then heads northwest, climbing to skirt the Vakhines peak, and offers incomparable views towards Cape Arnauti. The Adonis Trail heads in the opposite direction initially giving splendid views over the coastline southeast of the Baths of Aphrodite. I take you up to the 'decision point' then describe both trails. Whichever you choose, you're likely to come back and head the opposite way another day!

You need more than sandals or trainers for either experience, for while the routes are well marked and by no means severe, they do present some challenge to wind and limb, and the surfaces can be rocky or loose especially on their zigzag descents.

The walk starts at the Baths of Aphrodite, where both trails are clearly indicated by a wooden signpost. After viewing the pool where Aphrodite was said to sport with lovers, move out to the right as indicated and within a couple of minutes catch the unmistakeable perfume of goats. Drop down to the right, then turn left on a broad track. At about **10min** look for a path that zigzags up to the left. It is opposite a goat enclosure; if you've gone past that, you've gone too far.

Climb the zigzag, and at about **15min** observe a cairn on the left. Look across the goat enclosure to a small island with a cross, which commemorates a diver who lost his life near the island some years ago.

At signpost No 10 be sure to follow a zigzag to the right, and very soon come to signpost No 11. There are seats near here from where you can enjoy your first really good views over the coast. Walk through a clearing which is level for about 200m/yds, but ahead you'll see (and feel!) the trail rising sharply. It can be a sweat, but the pain doesn't last long! At the top there's a welcome bench from which to look back to Lachi and beyond to Polis.

Carry on along a stony track, and turn left after signpos No 20, opposite what I think is an old fire-watch 'chair' You will come to a wooded area which is excellent for picnicking. **This is where you have the choice of the Aphrodite or Adonis trails**... be here at **1h**, or maybe less

For Adonis (numbered B25 to B55), turn left immediately. Ahead is another nature trail arch (Smiyies; Walk 19). Look round to the right at the archaeological site of Pyrgos tis Rigaenas (Queen's Shelter), believed to be the site of a medieval monastery. To the right of this is the

View down to the Baths of Aphrodite from the end of the Adonis Trail

start of the Aphrodite Trail (numbered A25 to A49).

Aphrodite: The trail does some zigzagging to climb to signpost A37, from where you'll have a stunning view towards Cape Arnauti. This is literally the high point of the walk (about 360m/1200ft), which continues on a narrowing path and makes a tricky but not too difficult zigzag descent, to join the coastal path at around **1h 45min**. Take care on the descent where the surface is loose. You'll finish up back at the tourist pavilion in about **2h**, maybe a little more, but who's rushing? This is a marvellous walk at any time of year, but in spring you may have the bonus of spotting the Cyprus tulip.

Adonis: The trail climbs a short distance, past juniper trees. Near signpost No B29 a forest road swings round to the right, but ignore that and keep ahead. When you come to a signpost at B34, turn left. There's a water trough here, of alleged drinking quality, but you may prefer your bottle. There's a really lovely descent now, to the right of a gulley, and the whole area is covered with wild flowers in springtime. Simply follow the trail numbers (there's a long gap between B46 and B47). At B50 you come to a stunning viewpoint from where you can see your zigzag descent to the Baths of Aphrodite, which you should reach after **2h** or so.

19 AKAMAS GOLD

See map on reverse of touring map

Distance: 13km/8mi; 3h30min

Grade: moderate, with ascents of about 250m/820ft

Equipment: walking boots or stout shoes, sunhat, water, picnic, torch

How to get there and return: car or taxi to/from Neokhorio (via Lach

Short walk for motorists: Smiyies Nature Trail (6.5km/4mi return; 2h easy). Drive on the rough road out of Neokhorio to the Smiyies picni site (see notes paragraph 3 below) and start and end the walk there.

Even shorter walk for motorists: Do the Short walk above, but turn o the ridge track at nature trail signpost No 9, where there is a sign 'Smiyie 2km'.

Alternative walks: Below are just two possibilities from the many wal options in this area (see map on reverse of touring map). You will nee to take a taxi to both start and return.

1 Neokhorio — Smiyies — Aphrodite Trail — Baths of Aphrodit (13km/8mi; 3h15min; an additional climb of 100m/330ft). After visitin the mine (1h30min), regain the higher track and continue along it, the turn right at a military warning sign to link up with the Aphrodite Trai (Walk 18). When you reach it after 500m/yds, fork left to climb roun the Vakhines peak and then descend to the Baths. (You could also tur *right* on the trail and descend more directly to the Baths from Pyrgos ti Rigaenas.)

2 Neokhorio — Smiyies — Adonis Trail — Baths of Aphrodite (10km 6.2mi; 2h30min). From the mine, continue on the Smiyies Nature Trai and fork left, to join the Adonis Nature Trail in about 10min, near poir No B34. Keep ahead to descend to the Baths.

Is it a gold mine? Or was it just magnesium ore tha Cypriot miners extracted from the abandoned working we find on this grand route? Let's go see, but don't give up the day job yet! The real rewards on this day's outing are the magnificent views over Kolpos Khrysokhou (*Golden* Bay) and the Akamas Forest in the south. I have given the distance for motorists who start and finish the walk at Neokhorio, but if you're up to it, I urge you to consider one of the longer Alternative walks.

Start out at the church in Neokhorio. Walk west along the road to some water tanks on the edge of the village where the road reverts to track and forks (**10min**). Head right here, towards Ayios Minas. The left fork would take you to the goats of Androlikou (Walk 20)… another day perhaps? After some **40min** you come to the restored church of Ayios Minas, then at **50min** to the popular Smiyies picnic site (Picnic 19). Keep to the left of it, passing the start of an optional 3km/2mi (1h) return climb to the top of Pissouromouti peak for a magnificent view over the whole coast.

Come at **55min** to a T-junction of tracks on a ridge ('Route A' in the 4WD Options for Car tour 1 on page 24)

Some say this abandoned mine once produced gold... but old maps indicate magnesium. Whatever the end product, this is the old smelter. The galleried workings of the mine can be explored with care; take a torch, and don't go alone.

Turn right and start enjoying the views, firstly to the left, and later, in both directions. There'll likely be a welcome breeze, even on a hot day.

You'll shortly see the turn-off to a fire-watch station, then a signpost back to 'Smiyies 2km' on your right (the 'even shorter walk'). Keep ahead and look out, off to the right, for a level track skirting round the hillside. Ignore it, but then watch for a second track (signposted as a nature trail): it drops down sharply to the right. This leads to the abandoned mine workings (**1h30min**). On the left is the smelting furnace (what's left of it) and, to the right, entrances to the old mine's galleries. If you have a torch, it's possible to explore some of them for a short distance, but take care, and don't venture in there alone. No gold nuggets? I'm sorry!

You now have several options. For the main walk, follow the track that drops down to the left of the smelting furnace, then fork right on the Smiyies Nature Trail. This will bring you back to the picnic site at **2h40min** or so, and to Neokhorio at around **3h30min**.

For Alternative walk 2 keep ahead on the track at the left of the smelting furnace to reach the Adonis Trail. For Alternative walk 1, return to the upper track and proceed as described above to the Aphrodite Trail.

A great day's walking, whatever your choice of routes.

20 LACHI • ANDROLIKOU • NEOKHORIO

See map on reverse of touring map

Distance: 12km/7.4mi; 2h45min

Grade: quite easy, with ascents of about 350m/1150ft

Equipment: walking boots or stout shoes, sunhat, water, picnic

How to get there: car to Lachi, or to Polis (Timetable E4), the taxi to Lachi

To return: taxi from Neokhorio, back to your car, or to Polis for a bu (either pre-arrange, or telephone when you arrive)

Alternative walks

1 Lachi — Androlikou — Neokhorio — Baths of Aphrodite (17km 10.5mi; 4h; grade and access as main walk; telephone for a taxi fror the tourist pavilion at the Baths to return). Walk from Neokhorio acros the hillside to the Baths ('Loutra Aphroditis' on the map), as describe at the end of the notes on page 92.

2 If you're a *very* long-walk freak, turn left on reaching the edge c Neokhorio, instead of right, and pleasure yourself with any of th options described in Walk 19! Lachi — Androlikou — Smiyies — th old mine — Adonis Trail — Baths of Aphrodite is a magnificent rambl of about 22km/13.6mi; 6h.

The once-quiet fishing shelter of Lachi, 3km from Polis has expanded into a holiday villa area in recent years but it still retains much of its charm. There is not mucl walking to be enjoyed from here without a car journey first, but here is an interesting little outing... if you like goats.

Start out near the children's playground at the Polis end of Lachi, and cross the road. Follow a track that leads round the end of a row of villas, then behind them climbing sharply. It levels and leads inland. After a few hundred metres/yards, drop down to the right at a smal goat enclosure (you ain't seen *nothing* yet!) and head lef again on a lower track through fields. Come at abou **45min** to an open area, to the left of which is a stone crusher. Keep ahead, join a rough road and turn right.

This leads to the once-Turkish village of Androlikou,

achi harbour

vhich was abandoned during the Turkish occupation of he north of the island in 1974. The village is now home o a single Greek Cypriot family, a few sheep, a few pigs, ı few noisy dogs... and around 1000 goats. This is a village with atmosphere!

Come into the village at about **1h40min**. Turn left, then ight, past a small piggery where an elderly lady guardian of the swine may invite a small contribution if you photograph her animals. After you've inspected the old houses, aken your pictures, and assured the dogs that you're not Turkish, set out from the piggery on a rough road that eads all the way to Neokhorio. At about **2h** there's a sharp dip to a stream, then a few minutes later look over to the ight and see a cave. It may only be a hole in the hillside, but it shows every sign of being someone's home.

At **2h10min** there is a view northwards to the sea, after which the track dips again to the left, coming at **2h25min**

Gourds and vines of Cyprus

Androlikou (top), ancient olive tree, a wild pig (not seen on this walk, I hasten to assure you), and fruit trees of the Akamas

to a junction. Keep to the lower track which drops down to the right and then heads north towards the sea. At around **2h40min**, skirt a pleasant wooded valley to come to a junction of tracks on the edge of Neokhorio. You will have gained the ability on your recent travels to recognise the creatures on your right as goats. Turn right, walking past water tanks to the right, and at **2h45min** enter the village; it is of no great visual merit but does boast several tavernas and a public telephone.

For Alternative walk 1, turn *left* about 40m/yds beyond the tanks, on a track alongside a wall. Bear right at a fork, then walk to the bottom of a modest gorge, and climb up the other side. Do not turn right towards the sea, but turn left and start heading across the hillside, towards the Baths of Aphrodite. The way heads roughly northwest, past route indicators (white column No 19 and various blue and red waymarks). After a slight dip in the track, walk past an area of bushes and trees on your right and look out for white bollard No 3 at the foot of a tree. No more than 100m/yds beyond this, turn right and zigzag down to a lower track that takes you across a streambed. You meet the Adonis Nature Trail (Walk 18). Turn right to the Baths of Aphrodite.

21 KRITOU TERRA AND TERRA

Distance: 4km/2.5mi, 1h30min

Grade: easy descent and reascent of about 150m/500ft

Equipment: stout shoes, sunhat, water, picnic

How to get there and return: 🚗 to/from Kritou Terra (a detour on Car tour 1, page 23). Park near the taverna.

This is a lovely, short and very interesting stroll — easy to get to from Paphos, via Kathikas, or from the Lachi-Polis area via Drousha. It starts in the village of Kritou Terra from the restored village springs near the taverna.

Start out by walking into the village (*don't* go along the Terra road). Keep walking ahead, observing on the right a coffee shop with an external iron staircase, then on the left just beyond it, the old village mill with a vine

Terra

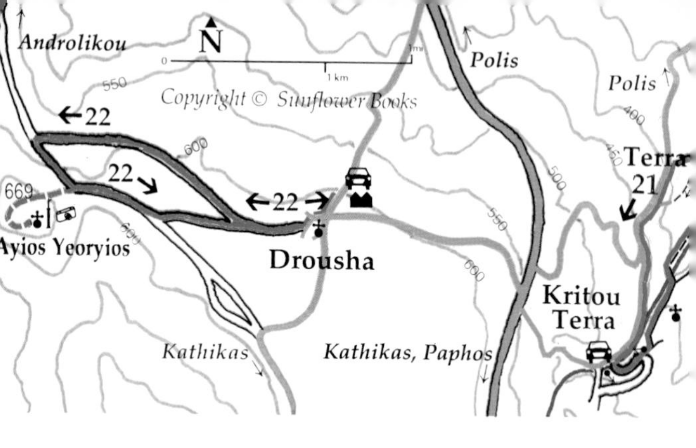

on its terraced roof. Beyond here is a low wall, over which you will see a series of holes in the rock beside a water channel. This was formerly the communal laundry.

The way drops a little, and you'll pass a small chapel on a rocky outcrop off to the right. Some 100m/yds further on, there is a metal grating in the road: turn left just beyond it, on an indistinct path (near a wooden gate). The path may be overgrown in places, and you should watch out for stones underfoot, especially after rain.

After crossing a streambed, the path widens out, and you now have an easy walk to Terra (**45min**) — among a myriad of wild flowers in springtime. Terra has a semi-derelict look... indeed many of its houses are unoccupied, but there has been a settlement here since Roman times. Nowadays some of the Turkish-owned houses abandoned during the 1974 occupation of the north are being restored by Greek tenants through a government conservation scheme.

Coming through Terra village, you will see the old mosque with cypress trees 'guarding' it. Linger a while in Terra, and maybe talk with a resident or two. It's a lovely peaceful place. Then bear left near the mosque and follow the road back to Kritou Terra (**1h 30min**). Visit the taverna near the entrance before you leave, and help keep a traditional Cypriot community thriving!

The Byzantine church of Ayia Ekaterina lies not far from Drousha and the Terras. Since this medieval ruin is more complete than many on Cyprus and contains some faded wall paintings, it is well worth a short (5km) detour during Car tour 1. To reach it, take the crudely-signposted road from Kritou Terra (not the Terra road). The church can also be reached within 2km from the Paphos/Polis road at a marked turn-off, 1km south of Skoulli.

22 DROUSHA

See map opposite

Distance: 6.5km/4mi; 2h

Grade: quite easy, with very little ascent

Equipment: walking boots or stout shoes, sunhat, water

How to get there and return: 🚗 to/from Drousha, or 🚌 to Polis (Timetable E4), then taxi to/from Drousha

The village of Drousha sits high amid the Akamas hills, and the views from it and the area round it are incomparable. This is a short but appealing walk, especially towards sunset — ideal for those of you staying in Drousha. You may be at the incongruously modern but well-sited Drousha Heights Hotel, which makes a good start to the walk, as well as a good base.

Start out by turning left from the hotel: walk slightly uphill into Drousha, passing Finikas Taverna. Then turn right between two coffee houses. Take the next left turn (before the theatre), then make a right after 100m/yds or so. This unmade road leads west out of the village. Once you are clear of all the buildings, keep right at a fork.

Observe the abandoned settlement of Pittokopos over to your right as the track first drops, then rises to a junction, where you should turn left (**1h**). After a few hundred metres/yards, come to an optional extra — a climb up the rocky hillside to your right where stands a modern chapel dedicated to St George (Ayios Yeoryios). This may not be exciting in itself, but the views certainly are.

Otherwise keep on the original track, stay left at a fork, and return to Drousha (**2h**), rejoining the road that led out of the village.

23 FROM LACHI TO AYIOS YEORYIOS, OR THE AUTHOR'S REVENGE!

Map begins on the reverse of the touring map, ends on pages 98-99

Distance: 27km/16.7mi; 7h

Grade: moderate, with ascents of about 300m/1000ft and a long descent of about 600m/2000ft

Equipment: walking boots or stout shoes, sunhat, plenty of water, picnic

How to get there: as Walk 20, page 90

To return: 🚗 telephone for a taxi when you arrive at Ayios Yeoryios (or arrange for friends to meet you)

Alternative walks: There are endless permutations. Masochists can combine this walk with Walks 13 or 14 — or parts of Walks 18-22; see maps on pages 94, 98-99 and the reverse of the touring map.

The Sunflower office tells me that some users of previous editions of *Landscapes of Cyprus* lamented the absence of a *really* long walk in the book. Well, this one is just for you! It isn't too difficult, but in the hot Cyprus sun you will need to carry plenty of water. There are no facilities of any kind on the route.

The good news is that much of the walk is level or downhill (albeit on rough tracks), and the views over the whole Lara coastline will linger long in the memory.

Start out by walking from Lachi to Androlikou, as described in the opening section of Walk 20 on page 90 (**1h40min**). But turn left and keep left when you enter the village; do not turn right at the pigs!

This way will take you across open country to the smaller and even more abandoned village of Fasli (**2h 30min**; from here refer to the map overleaf). The track swings right to approach it, then left to skirt round it. At about **3h** or less, come to a junction with a broader track, having observed the ruined settlement of Pittikopos over to your left. Turn right. (A left turn would take you into Drousha in around 45min, where you could join Walk 22.)

You now follow the roughest 'road' you're likely to find on Cyprus (4WD Option B in Car tour 1 bumps along here). After about 1km turn left (**3h15min**), to start gaining views over the whole western coast around Lara Bay which is slightly to the left on the horizon. That is your target!

The way is simple, but don't rush it. Relish this *totally* unspoiled region, listen to the birdsong, smell the air, and take some wonderful photos as you follow the winding track gently downwards for some 7km, to join the rough road above Lara. After visiting the beach (Walk 13), you have another 7km of walking on a similar road (past the turn-off to the Avagas Gorge and Walk 14). You should reach Ayios Yeoryios at about **7h**, depending on your

Both wild garlic (left) and wild geraniums flourish in stony areas and olive groves; they flower in late spring.

stride, and how many times you stop to take in the scenery. You'll be tired and thirsty, but you'll thank me for this wonderful experience of the Akamas... but perhaps not immediately!

Lara Beach in early spring

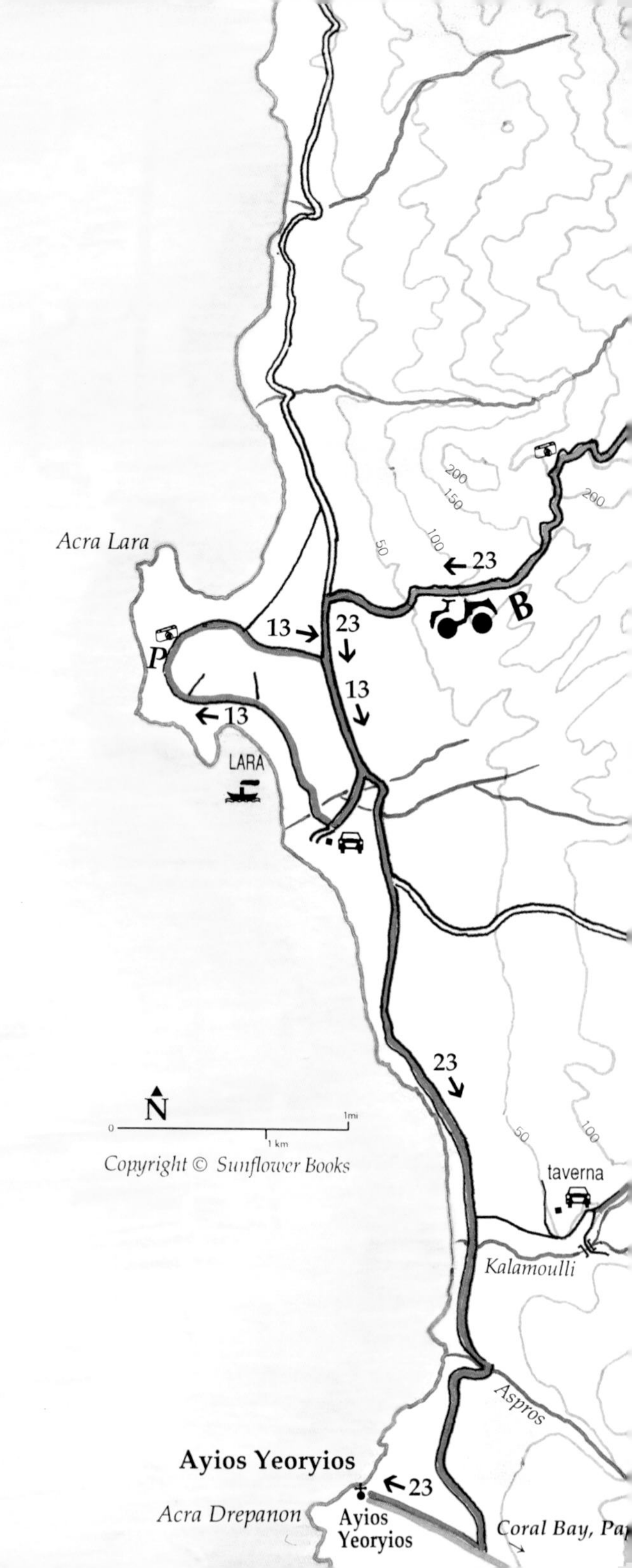

Acra Lara
P
13
23
13
23
B
200
150
100
50
200
13
LARA
23
N
0
1mi
1 km
Copyright © Sunflower Books
50
100
taverna
Kalamoulli
Aspros
Ayios Yeoryios
23
Acra Drepanon
Ayios
Yeoryios
Coral Bay, Pa

Smiyies
16-17
Androlikou (300 m)
20, 16-17
Fasli
23
Pittikopos
23
22, 94
Ayios Yeoryios
Droush
AGAS
Argaki tou Kouphou
350
400
450
500
550
600
200

24 ALAMANOU TO GOVERNOR'S BEACH

Distance: 6km/3.7mi; 1h45min (or 12km/7.4mi; 3h30min return)

Grade: very easy

Equipment: stout shoes, sunhat, water, swimwear

How to get there: taxi or car to Ayios Yeoryios Alamanou

To return: taxi from Governor's Beach — back to base, or back to your car. There is also a from Governor's Beach which runs to the waterfront hotels in Limassol between May and September: check up-to-date times with a tourist office.

If Governor's Beach were white or golden in colour, developers would have had their way with it by now. But its grey (though clean) appearance has saved this popular retreat from touristic blandness. No one would include it in a list of the world's great watering-holes, but its informal — even ramshackle — atmosphere makes for a happy start and/or finish to this easiest of strolls. The walk can be acomplished with ease in either direction, but hire-car drivers might find it most agreeable to start at the monastery of Ayios Yeoryios Alamanou, walk to Governor's Beach for a swim and lunch, then return. The monastery is not particularly ancient, but its blue and white galleries and courtyard are very pretty, as you can see in the photograph opposite.

Just before the monastery car park, there is a track off to the left which is where **the walk starts**. In about **30min** you reach the sea and a shingle beach, close to which you may find a cafe of sorts, in the high season. Turn left along the beach for a few minutes, then climb briefly onto a track which winds along to Governor's Beach, hugging the waterline. Your journey should take about **1h45min**.

At the headland of Cape Dolos you will look down over the Governor's Beach area, and the best approach from here is to head inland a little, to pick up the signposted track down to the tavernas, of which there are several to choose from.

Retrace your steps for a walk back to the monastery, or take a taxi if the effort of lunch has been too much!

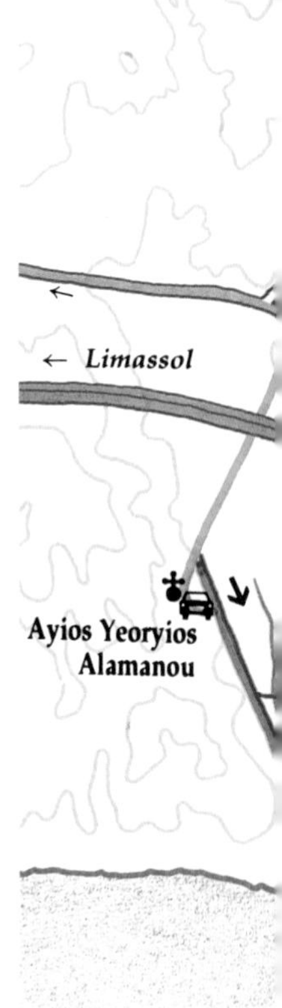

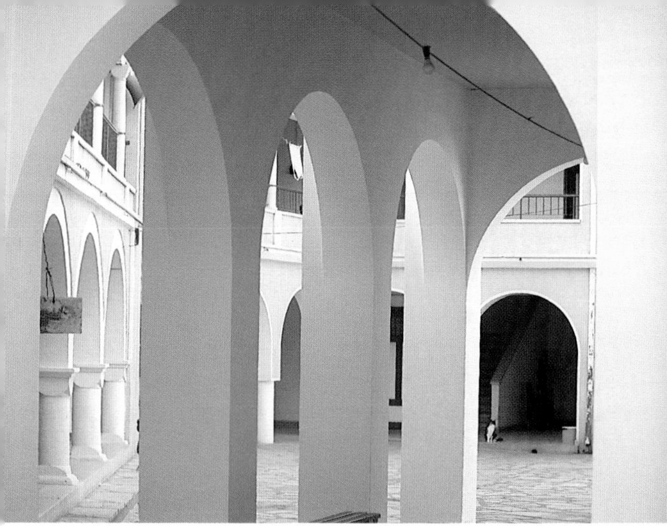

The blue and white galleries and courtyard at the monastery of Ayios Yeoryios Alamanou: the sisters here sell flowers, jam, eggs and chickens, and a lone monk occupies a single room near the entrance, wherein he eats, sleeps, and paints icons which the visitor can buy.

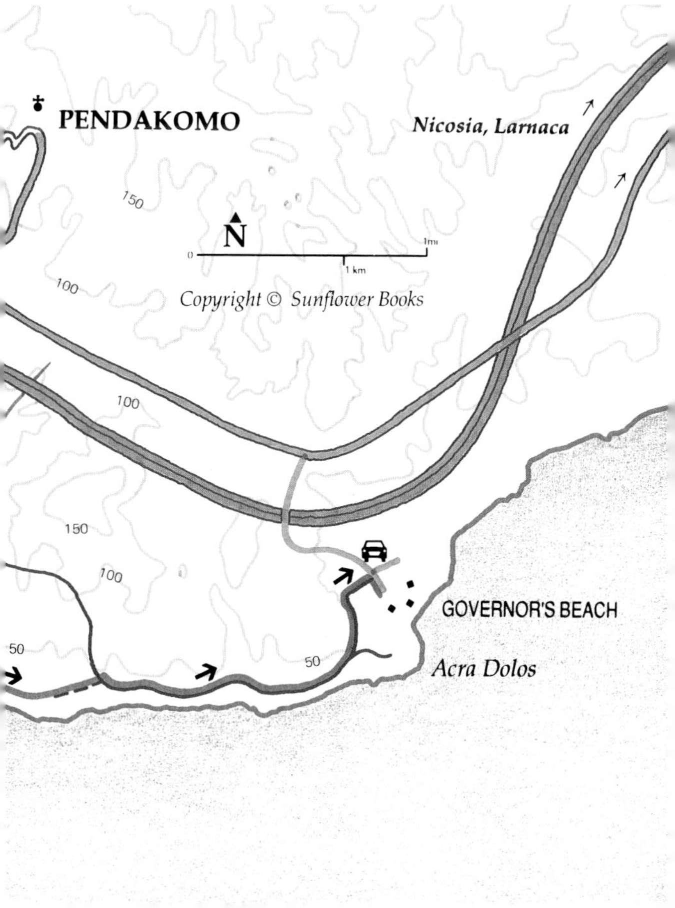
PENDAKOMO
Nicosia, Larnaca
150
N
0
1 km
1mi
100
Copyright © Sunflower Books
100
150
100
GOVERNOR'S BEACH
50
50
Acra Dolos

25 MT MAKHERAS

Distance: 6km/3.7mi;1h30min

Grade: moderate, with an ascent/descent of about 150m/500ft

Equipment: stout shoes, sunhat, water, picnic

How to get there and return: 🚗 only accessible by car (from Limassol via Kellaki and Ayii Vavatsinias — a very rough road; from Larnaca via Kalokhorio, Sha and Mathiati; from Nicosia via Analiondas). Park as described in the text. *NB: Tracks may be impassable in winter or early spring.*

Short walk: Drive up the rough road from the picnic site to where the scramble starts, but take care where and how you park on the narrow road.

This is a journey to the centre of Cyprus affords a stunning view in all directions after a short uphill walk and an energetic scramble along an easy ridge.

As one approaches Mount Makheras, from whatever direction, one becomes increasingly aware of the radar

Makheras Monastery, second in importance only to Kykko, was founded in 1148, but burned down in 1530 and again in 1892. Most of what the visitor sees today dates from 1900, but the monastery is a very peaceful and beautiful retreat, especially when the almond blossoms in February. Views from its terraces are quite impressive. In the 1950s, the EOKA organisation had a hide-out in a nearby cave, where second-in-command Gregoris Afxentiou died after a skirmish with British troops. The monastery, like Kykko, has a wealth of icons — including the one said to have inspired its founding.

weather station on its summit, perched like a huge golf ball on a giant tee. Below the peak, which is a few kilometres south of Makheras Monastery, is the Kionia picnic site, with tables, benches, and barbecue facilities.

This walk starts a little *north* of the picnic site, near a U-bend in the road to the monastery. Park on an old picnic site with fine views. Cross the road and immediately climb a short distance through trees and scrub. After **10min** or less, join the rough road and follow it uphill.

There is no reason why you should not go all the way to the top for the magnificent panorama seen from just outside the gates to the radar station. But the main walk continues from a point on the left of the road, less than 200m/yds below the gates near a gnarled tree, where you scramble briefly down from the road and head for the obvious ridge. Viewed from the tree, the scramble looks easier than it is, but it is not difficult for fit walkers.

After perhaps **30min** come to a cairn and, 500m/yds beyond that, another cairn — a point where one feels as if the whole of Cyprus is spread below in every direction. A beautiful high place (**45min**).

Retrace your steps to your car (**1h30min**), and perhaps call at Makheras Monastery, where there is a seasonal café.

26 STAVROVOUNI MONASTERY

See also photograph page 17

Distance: 4km/2.5mi; 2h

Grade: moderate ascent/descent of 300m/1000ft; avoid in wet weather

Equipment: stout shoes, sunhat, water, picnic

How to get there and return: 🚘 Stavrovouni makes a reasonable excursion from Larnaca by taxi, if sharing. Otherwise a hire car is essential. Park/alight at the 'Spithoudia' signpost (see below, paragraph 3).

***Special note**: Women are not allowed inside Stavrovouni or Ayia Varvara, nor is photography permitted, but the views from the car park are still superb.*

For no other reason than to experience the sheer magnificence of the views from the top (see photograph on page 17), the ascent to Stavrovouni, whether on foot or the easy way, is a must for anyone visiting Cyprus. A grand sweep of the eyes round all points of the compass takes in distant mountains, a whole spectrum of landscape colours and dozens of villages and vineyards.

On three sides, Stavrovouni ('Mountain of the Holy Cross') is almost sheer, but the fourth side is negotiable by the sturdy of foot. Approach is via the old Nicosia/Limassol road, or a turn-off from the new road. The last few miles are hardly a delight, distinguished by a stone-crushing plant and the high-profile presence of an army camp. 'No photography' signs abound. But once this is all behind you, the magic begins.

By car or taxi, head first for the smaller monastery of Ayia Varvara (bee-keeping and icon-painting) and a point several hundred metres beyond, where a sign indicates 'Spithoudia' to the right. Opposite here, to the left, is the **starting point of the walk**. Follow this track for about 100m/yds, to pass a small pumping station. A very short distance (no more than 40m/yds beyond the pumping station) look out for the start of a narrow path on your right, rising sharply from the track.

All you have to do now is climb steadily to heaven! The way is steep and rough and not always distinct, but a useful guide is to keep a narrow-gauge pipe which runs to the top in view. Progress is helped by an occasional levelling-off of the path. Some two-thirds of the way up, the path leads on to the motor road, leaving one little option but to follow this a short way, as it zigzags in its final approach to the summit (688m/2250ft). The ascent shouldn't take any more than **45min**, depending on your scrambling ability.

Your reward, at the top, is the finest panorama on Cyprus (Picnic 26). The monastery itself is worth looking

tavrovouni Monastery: entrance and icons

t, but it should be noted that women visitors are not llowed inside. Stavrovouni is regarded as the oldest onastery on Cyprus, founded by St Helena circa 330, nd among its artefacts is a piece of 'the true cross', now ncased in silver. The monks are not unwelcoming to nale) visitors, but they are a strict, ascetic group, more nterested in devotions than in running a tourist pavilion. ruit is sometimes available from a stall near the gate, and nere are toilet facilities.

The way back down is a choice of either retracing ne's footsteps or walking down the motor road. The full ircuit of Stavrovouni should take around **2h**, but more if ou linger at the top… and who would not?

27 AYIA NAPA • CAPE GRECO • PROTARAS

See also photograph page 18 **Distance**: 14km/8.7mi; 4

Grade: quite easy, but with tricky stretches over razor-sharp rocks

Equipment: boots (ankle protection is *essential*), sunhat, water, picni swimming things

How to get there: 🚌 to Ayia Napa (Timetable C5). Local buses als serve the Ayia Napa/Protaras/Paralimni area (Timetables D2-D4; re check times at a tourist office)

To return: 🚌 local Ayia Napa/Protaras/Paralimni (Timetables D2-D4

Short walk: This walk can be shortened at almost any point along i length by reaching the coast road and flagging down a bus, or callir for a taxi from any of the hotels.

The far reaches of any island always hold fascinatio for the traveller, and this southeastern corner c Cyprus is no exception. It is easily accessible too — Ayi Napa is one of the island's most popular tourist centre: This walk takes in sandy beaches, quiet coves, a radar topped headland and an attractively sited church.

Begin the walk in Ayia Napa, just north of the Grecia Sands Hotel (south of the Marina Hotel), where the roa swings round to the left. Follow the track that lead seawards, offering a pleasing view over Ayia Napa beac within two minutes. At this point there is no probler establishing which way to go. Simply keep close to th sea and head eastwards (Picnic 27), experiencing littl

The walk from Ayia Napa to Cape Greco reveals interesting sea caves east of Kermia Beach. This view is from the east, looking back towards the start of the walk. Some hotels at Ayia Napa can just be seen on the horizon. If you want to picnic over-looking these caves, you must wear stout shoes and be sure to take something soft to sit on; the rocks are very sharp!

andy beaches, rocky inlets and, at about **40min**, Kermia Beach and its apartments. A few minutes beyond here, he going gets tricky. No longer is there the luxury of a clear track. A faint path of sorts marks the way ahead but even this disappears after a while. Underfoot the rocks are sharp-edged. It is not difficult to pick a way through hem, but great care should be taken to avoid ankle injury. Progress here will be slower. Look out for inlets where waves crash into sea caves (see below). At around **h15min**, perhaps sooner, you will approach the dominant headland which has been in view throughout the walk. Better here to move away from the sea, and join a path which skirts its base.

A worthwhile detour (or an alternative ending to the walk) is to enjoy the Forestry Department nature trail on he headland. This offers splendid views over Cape Greco and along to Ayia Napa. Join the trail by heading inland on the aproach to the headland instead of keeping to the lower path. From the top of the headland to the main road where you can catch a bus is about 1km.

If you are pressing on to Cape Greco, keep to (or rejoin) he lower path at the base of the headland, round it, then catch a first glimpse of the cape with its lighthouse and he relay masts of Radio Monte Carlo. A little further on,

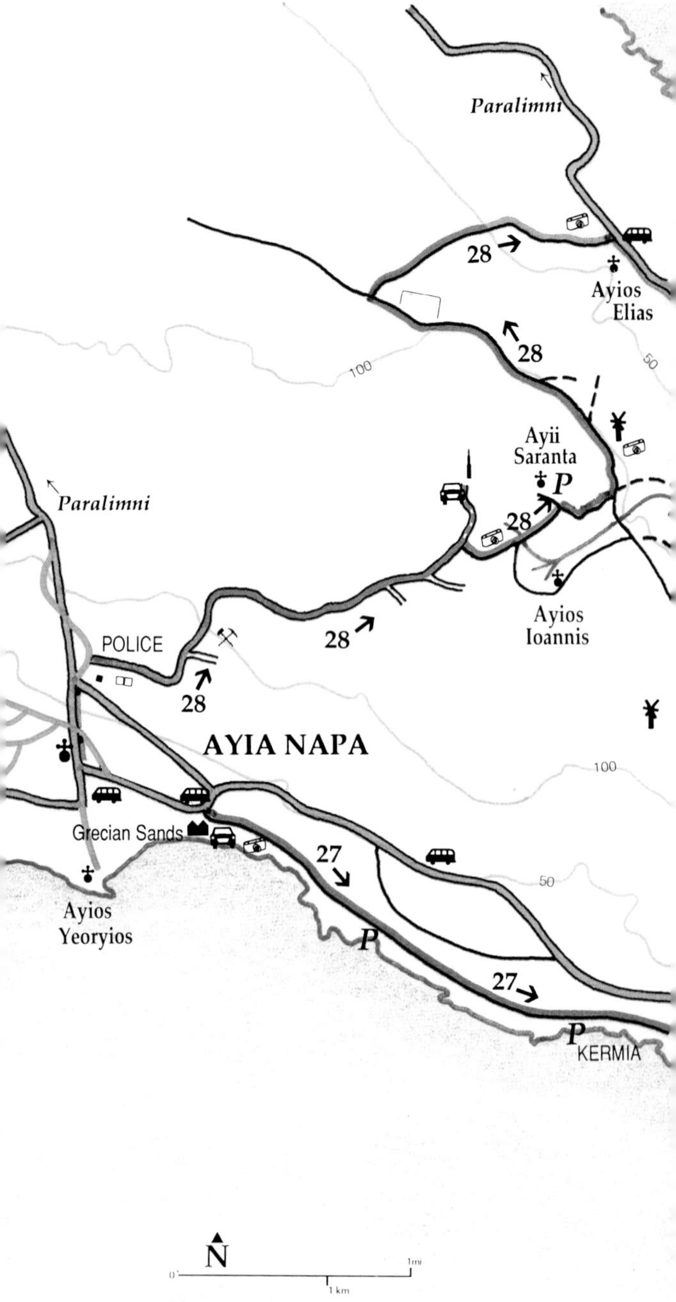

Paralimni
28
Ayios Elias
28
100
50
Ayii Saranta
P
28
Paralimni
POLICE
28
28
Ayios Ioannis
AYIA NAPA
100
Grecian Sands
27
50
Ayios Yeoryios
P
27
P
KERMIA
N
0
1 km
1mi

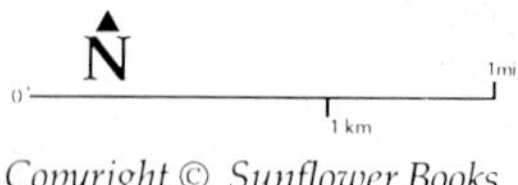

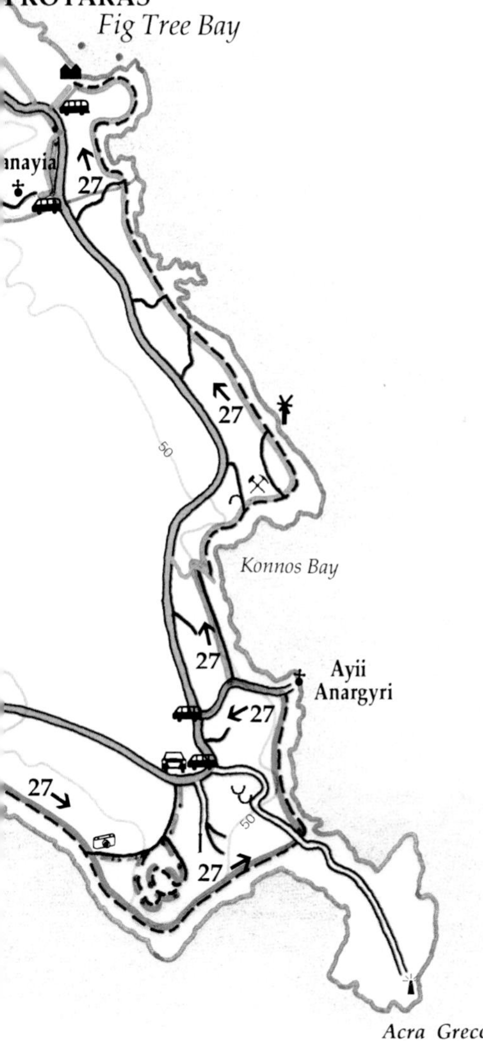
PROTARAS
Fig Tree Bay
anayia
27
27
50
Konnos Bay
27
Ayii
Anargyri
27
27
50
27
Acra Greco

look to a military radar installation high on the left. Keep well to the right of a cultivated area and climb a low hill, beyond which is a path leading down to the Cape Greco road. You can turn right here to get closer to the radio masts, but a locked gate prevents access to the cape itself.

It is easier to make for the eastern side of the cape and head for the picturesque little church of Ayii Anargyri (**2h**). From here, head up the rough road that leads to the main road and end the walk by catching a bus back to Ayia Napa here if you wish. Otherwise, look for a track off to the right, leading along the edge of a not-very-high cliff, to sandy Konnos Bay (visible from Ayii Anargyri). At about **2h15min** come to a road zigzagging down to the bay, but before reaching the beach cross a bridge on the left (signposted) and follow a track overlooking the beach. This track soon peters out on a rock-strewn hillside.

But 'Landscapers' do not worry about small problems like this! They keep going, guide in hand, clambering over rocks, following the vaguest of paths which at first dips towards the sea (just beyond the sand) and then climbs the hillside again, to a levelling-off point from which there are pleasing views back over Konnos Bay towards Cape Greco. Some miles off the cape there is believed to lie the wreck of a 15th-century Genoese ship, as yet undiscovered.

Walk through an area of rock falls and dead trees with another, more rocky bay down to the right, and come shortly to a distinct track. Bear left for a moment to observe a cave in the hillside, but return to follow the edge of a cliff, skirting a cultivated area (**2h45min**). Vertigo is a small risk, but easily avoided. Within a minute or two you may feel that the way ahead is at first sight impossible.

Nonsense! It is just an old quarry that represents a modest challenge to the nimble-footed. The way through is far from distinct, so pick your own best route through this miniature 'lost world' of boulders and undergrowth, emerging at a level area on the far side. A broad track bears left, but keep seawards for a minute or two, then turn left to walk parallel with the shore, about 100m/yds inland. To the left are a few houses, ahead is a windmill, and away to the right a jagged, rocky area leading to the sea. Explore it if you wish, but watch your ankles!

From here, progress is over a completely flat coastal strip, leading at **4h** or less to Protaras, depending on when you call it a day. You will walk through farmland, over rocks, and round sandy inlets — a relatively unspoiled corner of Cyprus which has a lot of charm.

28 AYIA NAPA • AYIOS ELIAS • PROTARAS

See map pages 108-109; see also photos pages 18, 36-37, 41, cover

Distance: 8km/5mi; 2h **Grade**: quite easy; little climbing

Equipment: walking boots or stout shoes, sunhat, water, picnic

How to get there: 🚌 to Ayia Napa (Timetable C5). Local buses also serve the Ayia Napa/Protaras/Paralimni area (Timetables D2-D4; re-check times at a tourist office)

To return: 🚌 local Ayia Napa/Protaras/Paralimni (Timetables D2-D4)

Short walk: Ayii Saranta (2km/1.2mi; 45min return). 🚗 drive the first part of the walk, along the rough road, and park short of the transmitter tower. Then use the notes below from the 35min- to the 50min-point.

This walk explores the gentle agricultural hills behind Ayia Napa and Protaras. Prise yourself away from the golden beaches and you'll find that some modest exertion reveals a different world... of wind-powered wells, rich red soil producing a harvest of vegetables, quaint little churches, and a few stony tracks waiting to be explored.

The walk can be done in either direction, but it is easier to locate the **start at Ayia Napa**. From the centre, walk north on the Paralimni road, and turn right just past the police station on a rough road that leads in **10min** or less to the community sport stadium. Turn left soon after passing this, and continue round the edge of a quarry. By now you should be seeing a radio transmitter mast in the middle distance. Keep heading towards it. A short distance from the mast, at about **35min**, the track makes a definite left turn. At this point, you should turn off right through an area of low trees and come to an open area from where there are views to Cape Greco.

To the left you should be able to pick out the dome and cross of Ayii Saranta (**50min**; Picnic 28). This most unusual, tiny church is set in a cave, and its only light comes from the dome on the hillside above it (see cover photograph). Inside you will find evidence of a

Walks 27 and 28 take you through 'windmill valley' — the rich agricultural flatlands around Protaras.

Windsurfer at Protaras; below: Cyprus thistle

latter-day icon painter at work, and the familar candles.

Continue beyond Ayii Saranta to join a broader track and head left alongside several of the windmills that are so vital to irrigation in this part of the world. At **1h05min** or less you should be getting views to the right of the imposing church of Ayios Elias on its rocky perch. Keep to the track, with the transmitter mast away to the left, and come to a fenced-off area. Some 300m/yds beyond it, turn right and follow the track through villa development to Ayios Elias and Protaras. Views from the church and its pedestal are pleasing; the church is modern but very attractive inside and out (see photogaph pages 36-37).

From Ayios Elias (**2h**), descend a short distance to the main coast road and pick up a bus or taxi if you need it.

SERVICE TAXI AND BUS TIMETABLES

Below are some destinations you may wish to visit by public transport. The number after the place name is the **timetable number**. Timetables follow on the next 12 pages, but do remember to get a current timetable from a bus station or tourist information office when you visit the island. Departure points for buses and service taxis are shown on the town plans (see pages 8-13) and on the walking maps.

Agros — Limassol B10
Amathus — Limassol B11
Ayia Napa (Agia Napa)
 — Larnaca C5, D1
 — Nicosia A8
 — Paralimni D4
Coral Bay — Paphos E7
Galata
 — Limassol B11
 — Nicosia A6
Kakopetria
 — Nicosia A6
Kalopanayiotis — Nicosia A5
Kiti — Larnaca C7
Kouklia — Paphos E8
Larnaca (Larnaka)
 all destinations C1 — C10
 — Ayia Napa C5, D1
 — Kiti C7
 — Limassol B2, B6, C2, C4
 — Nicosia A1, A3, C1, C3
 — Paralimni C6, D2
 — Pervolia C8
 — tourist beaches C9, C10
Limassol (Lemesos)
 all destinations B1 — B11
 — Agros B10
 — Amathus B11
 — Larnaca B2, B6, C2, C4
 — Nicosia A2, A4
 — Paphos B3, B5, E1, E3
 — Pedhoulas B9
 — Platres B7, B8, B9
 — Prodhromos B9
Nicosia (Lefkogia)
 all destinations A1 — A8
 — Ayia Napa A8
 — Kakopetria A6
 — Larnaca A1, A3, C1, C3
 — Limassol A2, A4, B1, B4
 — Platres A5
 — Troodos A7
Panayia — Paphos E9
Paphos (Pafos)
 all destinations E1 — E11
 — Coral Bay E7
 — Kouklia E8
 — Limassol B3, B5, E1, E3
 — Panayia E9
 — Polis E2, E4
 — Pomos E10
 — Pyrgos E11
 — Yeroskipos E5, E6
Paralimni
 — Ayia Napa D4
 — Larnaca C6, D2
 — Protaras D3
Paramali
 — Limassol B3
 — Paphos E3
Pedhoulas
 — Limassol B9
 — Nicosia A5
Pervolia — Larnaca C8
Petra tou Romiou
 — Limassol B3
 — Paphos E3
Pissouri
 — Limassol B3
 — Paphos E3
Platres
 — Limassol B7 — B9
 — Nicosia A5
Polis — Paphos E2, E4
Pomos — Paphos E10
Prodhromos
 — Limassol B9
 — Nicosia A5
Protaras
 — Ayia Napa D4
 — Paralimni D3
Pyrgos — Paphos E11
Troodos — Nicosia A7
Yeroskipos — Paphos E5, E6

No	Itinerary	Company	Address or Location

Services from NICOSIA (Lefkosia)

SERVICE TAXIS

No	Itinerary	Company	Address or Location
A1	**Nicosia to LARNACA** (three operators, all operating same timetable)	Acropolis Kyriakos Makris	9 Stasinou 27 Stasinou 11 Stasinou
A2	**Nicosia to LIMASSOL** (four operators, all operating same timetable)	Karydas Kypros Kyriakos Makris	8 Omirou 9A Stasinou 27 Stasinou 11 Stasinou

Nicosia to PAPHOS — *Service is via Limassol; see Timetable B3*

BUS SERVICES — INTERCITY

No	Itinerary	Company	Address or Location
A3	**Nicosia to LARNACA**	Lefkaritis	6 Stasinou
A4	**Nicosia to LIMASSOL**	Kemek	34 Leonidou (near Solomos Sq)

Nicosia to PAPHOS — *Service is via Limassol; see Timetable B5*

BUS SERVICES — RURAL AND SUBURBAN

No	Itinerary	Company	Address or Location
A5	**Nicosia to PLATRES** (via Kalopanayiotis—Moutoullas—Pedhoulas—Prodhromos)	Zingas, c/o Kemek	34 Leonidou (near Solomos Sq)
	PLATRES to Nicosia	Kemek	Kemek, Platres
A6	**Nicosia to KAKOPETRIA**	Clarios	Station, Costanza Bastion, (200m east of Eleftheria Sq)
	KAKOPETRIA to Nicosia	Clarios	Kakopetria village
A7	**Nicosia to TROODOS**	Clarios	see A6
	TROODOS to Nicosia	Clarios	Troodos
A8	**Nicosia to AYIA NAPA** (four operators)	EMAN	100m east of post office in Eleftheria Sq
		un-named	Solomos Square
		Deryneia	27 Stasinou (c/o Kyriako
	AYIA NAPA to Nicosia	EMAN	as D1, page 120
		un-named	Ayia Napa harbour
		Deryneia	enquire at tourist office

Telephone No	Timetable
02-472525 02-444141 02-466201	*Daily,* every half hour from 06.00 to 18.00 (19.00 in summer)
02-462269 02-464811 02-444141 02-466201	*Winter* *Daily,* every half hour from 05.30 to 18.30 *Summer* *Daily,* every half hour from 05.30 to 19.00
02-442566	*Monday to Friday:* 08.30, 10.30, 13.00, 14.30, 16.00, 17.45 *Saturdays:* 14.30
02-463989	*Monday to Friday:* 06.30, 07.30, 09.00, 12.00, 14.00, 16.00 *Saturdays:* 07.00, 10.00, 14.30
02-463154	*Weekdays only:* 12.15
	Weekdays only: 06.00
02-453234	*Monday to Saturday:* 06.10, 10.20, 11.30, 13.10, 14.00, 14.30, 15.30, 16.00, 16.15, 16.45, 17.30 (18.30, 19.00 in summer) *Sundays:* 08.00, 18.00 *(July and August)* *Monday to Saturday:* 05.20, 05.45, 06.10, 06.30, 08.00, 13.30, 14.30 *Sundays:* 06.00, 16.30 *(July and August)*
02-453234	*Weekdays only:* 11.30 *Weekdays only:* 06.30
03-721321	*Weekdays only:* 15.00
02-473414	*Sundays only, mid-June to mid-Sept:* 09.00
02-444141	*Weekdays only:* 13.30
03-721321	*Monday to Saturday:* 08.00
02-473414	*Sundays only, mid-June to mid-Sept:* 17.00
03-821318	*Weekdays only:* approx. 08.00; *enquire!*

No	Itinerary	Company	Address or Location

Services from LIMASSOL (Lemesos)

SERVICE TAXIS

No	Itinerary	Company	Address or Location
B1	**Limassol to NICOSIA** (four operators, all operating same timetable)	Karydas Kypros Kyriakos Makris	21 Thessalonikis 193 Chris Hadjipavlo[u] 21 Thessalonikis 166 Ellados
B2	**Limassol to LARNACA** (two operators, both operating same timetable)	Acropolis Makris	49 Sp Araouzou 166 Elladhos
B3	**Limassol to PAPHOS** (four operators, all operating same timetable)	Karydas Makris Kyriakos Nea Paphos	21 Thessalonikis 166 Ellados 21 Thessalonikis 1 Vragadinou

BUS SERVICES — INTERCITY

No	Itinerary	Company	Address or Location
B4	**Limassol to NICOSIA** (two operators)	Kemek Costas	Corner Irinis & Enoseos Streets 9B Thessalonikis
B5	**Limassol to PAPHOS** (two operators)	Kemek Costas	same as B4 same as B4
B6	**Limassol to LARNACA**	Kallenos c/o Kemek	Corner Irinis & Enoseos Streets

BUS SERVICES — RURAL AND SUBURBAN

No	Itinerary	Company	Address or Location
B7	**Limassol to PLATRES**	Kyriakos/ Karydas	21 Thessalomikis
	PLATRES to Limassol	Kyriakos/ Karydas	Platres
B8	**Limassol to PLATRES**	(mini-bus)	21 Thessalonikis (c/o Karydas Taxis)
	PLATRES to Limassol	(mini-bus)	Platres
B9	**Limassol to PLATRES, TROODOS and PRODHROMOS**	Kemek	corner of Irinis & Enoseos Streets
	PRODHROMOS , TROODOS and PLATRES to Limassol	Kemek	Prodhromos Troodos Platres
B10	**Limassol to AGROS**	Agros Bus	c/o Kemek (same as B9)
	AGROS to Limassol	Agros Bus	Agros village

Continues on the next page

hone	Timetable
05-362061	*Winter*
05-363979	*Daily,* every half hour from 06.00 to 18.00
05-364114	*Summer*
05-365550	*Daily,* every half hour from 06.00 to 19.00
05-366766	*Daily,* every half hour from 06.00 to 18.00
05-365550	(19.00 in summer)
05-362061	
05-365550	*Daily,* every half hour from 06.00 to 18.00
05-364114	(19.00 in summer)
05-355355	
05-363241	*Monday to Friday:* 06.30, 09.00, 14.00, 16.00
	Saturdays: 07.00, 12.00, 14.30
05-354394	*Mon/Tue/Thur/Fri:* 09.30, 10.30; *Sat:* 09.30
same as B4	*Monday to Saturday:* 09.30
same as B4	*Mon/Tue/Thur/Fri:* 13.30, 17.00; *Wed/Sat:* 14.00
05-363241	*Monday to Friday:* 08.00, 10.00, 14.00, 16.00
	Saturdays: 08.00, 13.00
05-362061 or	*Weekdays only:* 11.30
05-364114	
	Weekdays only: 07.00
05-362061	*may be discontinued; enquire at bus operator*
05-362061	*may be discontinued; enquire at bus operator*
05-363241	*Monday to Saturday:* 14.00
05-363241	*Monday to Saturday:* departs Prodhromos 05.00, departs Troodos 05.30, departs Platres 06.00
same as B9	*Monday to Saturday:* 11.50
	Monday to Saturday: 07.00

No	Itinerary	Company	Address or Location
B11	**Limassol to AMATHUS**	EAL	main bus stop, Limassol market
	AMATHUS to Limassol	EAL	Hotel Meridien

Services from LARNACA

SERVICE TAXIS

No	Itinerary	Company	Address or Location
C1	**Larnaca to NICOSIA** (three operators, all operating same timetable)	Acropolis	Corner Gr Afxendiou & Makariou
		Kyriakos	2C Ermou
		Makris	13 Vasileos Pavlou
C2	**Larnaca to LIMASSOL** (two operators, both operating same timetable)	Acropolis	Corner Gr Afxendiou & Makariou III
		Makris	13 King Paul Street

Larnaca to PAPHOS — *Service is via Limassol; see Timetable B3*

BUS SERVICES — INTERCITY

No	Itinerary	Company	Address or Location
C3	**Larnaca to NICOSIA**	Kallenos	bus stop opposite the Four Lanterns Hotel
C4	**Larnaca to LIMASSOL**	Kallenos	bus stop opposite the Four Lanterns Hotel

Larnaca to PAPHOS — *Service is via Limassol; see Timetable B5)*

BUS SERVICES — RURAL AND SUBURBAN

No	Itinerary	Company	Address or Location
C5	**Larnaca to AYIA NAPA**	EMAN	bus stop opposite the Four Lanterns Hotel
	AYIA NAPA to Larnaca	EMAN	Ayia Napa bus station, between monastery square and the harbour
C6	**Larnaca to PARALIMNI**	Paralimni-Deryneia	bus stop opposite police station, Makariou
	PARALIMNI to Larnaca	Paralimni-Deryneia	Ag Georgios Sq in Paralimni, or from hotel area, Protaras

Continues on the next page

elephone No	Timetable
	Buses 6 and 30 operate year round between the town and the hotels to the east, along the coast road; enquire about times at a tourist office
04-655555 04-655100 04-652929	*Daily,* every half hour from 06.00 to 18.00 (19.00 in summer)
04-655555 04-652929	*Daily,* every half hour from 06.00 to 18.00 (19.00 in summer)
04-654890 or 05-654850	*Monday to Friday:* 06.30, 08.00, 09.00, 10.30, 13.00, 14.30, 16.00 *Saturdays:* 07.00, 09.00, 11.00, 13.00
04-654890 or 05-654850	*Monday to Friday:* 08.00, 10.00, 13.00, 16.00 *Saturdays:* 08.00, 13.00
	Monday to Saturday: 08.30, 09.30, 10.30, 11.30, 13.00, 14.00, 15.30, 16.30 (17.30 in summer) *Sundays, May to October only:* 08.30, 10.30, 13.00, 16.30
	Monday to Saturday: 08.00, 09.00*, 10.00, 11.00*, 12.00, 14.00, 15.00*, 16.00, 17.00* *these buses run May to October only *Sunday, May to October:* 09.00, 11.00, 15.00, 16.00
03-821318	*Monday to Friday:* 08.00, 10.00, 12.00, 13.30, 14.30, 16.30, 17.00, (18.00 from May to October), *Saturdays:* 08.00, 10.00, 12.00, 13.00, 15.00
03-821318	*Monday to Friday:* 08.00, 09.00, 10.00, 13.30, 15.00, (16.00 from May to October) *Saturdays:* 08.00, 09.00, 10.30, 13.30

No	Itinerary	Company	Address or Location
	Larnaca to PROTARAS — *Service is via Paralimni; see Timetable C6 above; see also Timetable D2*		
C7	**Larnaca to KITI** (Angeloktisti Church)	'No 19' Bus	Ayios Lazaros Square
	KITI to Larnaca	'No 19' Bus	Kiti village
C8	**Larnaca to PERVOLIA**	Pervolia	Ayios Lazaros Square
	PERVOLIA to Larnaca	Pervolia	Pervolia village
C9	**Larnaca to TOURIST BEACH EAST of Larnaca**	(beach bus)	next to Larnaca Tourist Office-
	TOURIST BEACH EAST to Larnaca	(beach bus)	tourist beach east of Larnaca
C10	**Larnaca to TOURIST BEACH WEST of Larnaca**	(beach bus)	same as C9
	TOURIST BEACH WEST to Larnaca	(beach bus)	tourist beach west

Services from Ayia Napa, Paralimni, Protaras

No	Itinerary	Company	Address or Location
D1	**Ayia Napa to LARNACA**	EMAN	bus station between monastery square and the harbour
	LARNACA to Ayia Napa: *see Timetable C5*		
D2	**Paralimni to LARNACA**	Paralimni-Deryneia	Ag Georgios Sq, Paralimni
	LARNACA to Paralimni: *see Timetable C6*		
D3	**Paralimni to PROTARAS and AYIA NAPA**	Paralimni-Deryneia	Ag Georgios Sq, Paralimni
	AYIA NAPA and PROTARAS to Paralimni	Paralimni-Deryneia	between monastery square and harbour
D4	**AYIA NAPA to Paralimni**	EMAN-	Dome and Asterias Hotel
	PARALIMNI Ayia Napa	EMAN	Ag Georgios Sq

elephone No	Timetable
	Monday to Saturday: 06.40, 08.00, 09.00, 10.00, 11.00, 12.00, 13.05, (14.00 Sat), 15,20, 16.10, 16.30, 17.00, 17.45, (19.00 in summer) *Monday to Saturday:* 06.10, 07.00, 07.40, 08.40, 09.40, 10.40, 11.40, 12.40, (13.40 Sat), 15.00, 16.00, 17.00
	Monday to Saturday: 06.30, 08.00, 10.00, 12.00, (13.45 Sat), 16.30, 17.45 *Monday to Saturday:* 08.30, 10.30, (13.00 Sat), 15.30, 17.00
	Monday to Friday: every half hour from 07.30 to 18.00 *Saturday:* every half hour from 08.00 to 17.00 *Sunday:* every hour from 08.00 to 16.00 as above
	enquire at the Larnaca Tourist Office
	enquire at the Larnaca Tourist Office
)3-721321	*Monday to Saturday, May to October:* 08.00, 09.00*, 10.00, 11.00*, 12.00, 14.00, 15.00*, 16.00, 17.00* *Sundays:* 09.00, 11.00, 15.00, 16.00 *these buses run May to October only
)3-821318	*Monday to Friday:* 08.00, 09.00, 10.30, 13.30, 15.00, (16.00 May to October only) *Saturdays:* 08.00, 09.00, 10.30, 13.30
)3-821318	*Daily, May to October:* 09.00*, 10.00, 11.00*, 12.00, 13.00*, 14.00, 16.00*, 17.00, 18.00*, 19.00 *not on Sundays *enquire at the tourist office*
)3-721321	*Monday to Saturday:* 09.00, 10.00, 11.00, 12.00, 13.00, 14.00, 16.00, 17.00, (18.00, 19.00 May-October only) *Sundays:* 09.00, 11.00, 13.00, 16.00, 18.00 *enquire at the tourist office*

No	Itinerary	Company	Address or Location

Services from PAPHOS

SERVICE TAXIS

No	Itinerary	Company	Address or Location
E1	**Paphos to LIMASSOL** (five operators, all same timetable)	Karydas	9 Evagora Pallikaridis
		Kypros	134 Makariou
		Kyriakos	9 Evagora Pallikaridis
		Nea Paphos	19 Evagora Pallikaridis
		Makris	19 Evagora Pallikaridis
E2	**Paphos to POLIS***	Karydas	9 Evagora Pallikaridis

**Service may be suspended; enquire in advance*

Paphos to NICOSIA — *Service is via Limassol; see Timetable B1*

Paphos to LARNACA — *Service is via Limassol; see Timetable B2*

BUS SERVICES — INTERCITY

No	Itinerary	Company	Address or Location
E3	**Paphos to LIMASSOL** (two operators)	Costas	28 Nicodemou Mylona (near the market)
		Amoroza/ Kemek	79 Evagora Pallikaridis (near the main square)
E4	**Paphos to POLIS**	Amoroza	79 Evagora Pallikaridis (near the main square)
	POLIS to Paphos	Amoroza	Polis centre

Paphos to NICOSIA — *Service is via Limassol; see Timetable B4*

Paphos to LARNACA — *Service is via Limassol; see Timetable B6*

BUS SERVICES — RURAL AND SUBURBAN

No	Itinerary	Company	Address or Location
E5	**Paphos to YEROSKIPOS**	'No 2' Bus	Paphos Post Office
	YEROSKIPOS to Paphos	'No 2' Bus	Yeroskipos centre
E6	**Paphos to YEROSKIPOS TOURIST BEACH** (via harbour area)	'No 11' Bus	Paphos Post Office
	TOURIST BEACH to Paphos (via the harbour)	'No 11' Bus	Yeroskipos Tourist Beach
E7	**Paphos to CORAL BAY**	ALEPA	Karavella station or the market
	CORAL BAY to Paphos	ALEPA	Coral Bay

Telephone No	Timetable
06-232459 06-237722 06-232424 06-232376 06-232538	*Daily,* every half hour from 06.00 to 18.00 (19.00 in summer)
061-32459	*Daily:* 10.00, 16.00
06-241717	*Mon/Tue/Thur/Fri:* 08.00, 09.00 *Wed/Sat:* 08.00
06-236822 or 06-236740	*Monday to Friday:* 14.30 *Saturdays:* 13.00
06-236822 or 06-236740	*Monday to Friday:* 06.30, 09.00, 10.00, 11.00 (Pomos), 12.00, 13.00, 14.00 (Pomos), 16.00 (Pomos), 17.00, 18.00 (Pomos), 19.00 (May to September) *Saturdays:* 09.00, 10.00, 11.00 (Pomos), 14.30 (Pomos), 16.00 (Pomos)
06-321114/5	*Monday to Friday:* 05.30, 06.30, 08.00, 09.30, 11.00, 12.00, 13.45, 14.30, 16.00, 17.00 *Saturdays:* 05.40, 07.30, 10.00, 12.00, 13.15, 14.30
	enquire at the Paphos Tourist Office (not included in Cyprus Tourism timetables)
	enquire at the Paphos Tourist Office (not included in Cyprus Tourism timetables)
06-234410	*enquire at the Paphos Tourist Office* (not included in Cyprus Tourism timetables)

No	Itinerary	Company	Address or Location
E8	**Paphos to KOUKLIA** (Temple of Aphrodite)	Kouklia Bus	same as E7
	KOUKLIA to Paphos	Kouklia Bus	Kouklia village
E9	**Paphos to PANAYIA** (Chrysorroyiatissa)	Panayia Bus	same as E7
	PANAYIA to Paphos	Panayia Bus	Panayia village
E10	**Paphos to POMOS**	Pomos Bus	same as E7
	POMOS to Paphos	Pomos Bus	Pomos village
E11	**Paphos to PYRGOS**	Pyrgos Bus	same as E7
	PYRGOS to Paphos	Pyrgos Bus	Pyrgos village

STOP PRESS

WALKS

Walk 10: Access: One can take Alepa bus 4 (Paphos to Tala; departs 09.30, 12.00) and walk 2km to the monastery. At the end of the walk there are buses from Tala at 15.00 and 17.00 (Mon-Thu) or 15.30, 17.00 (Fri). (User, 6/00) • At the **start** we turn sharp left 50m/yds before an old stone warehouse. You don't see any vineyards here; you only see them after passing the fork to the radio aerials (**45min**). (User, 3/00) • After the **1h**-point we turn left on a road after the second sign to Kili. This leads *into a new housing development. At the end of the estate, turn left downhill on a track through vineyards.* Then, after about 25m/yds, look out on the left for a narrow, indistinct stony path, rather overgrown with thorny bushes. *If you come to a fence, walk left along it until you reach the track.* (User, 6/00)

Walk 11, IMPORTANT: This walk is no longer possible as described in the book, because of the military base. However, a user who winters annually in Cyprus has sent in a variation which visits the dam. His version is a bit longer than Geoff's, but he does not give the exact time. If you start at Kissonerga (as in the book) and follow Geoff's instructions from the dam (instead of the longer version described below), the walk should not take more than about 2h30min. 'Take the Coral Bay bus and alight at the Cynthiana Beach Hotel. Cross the road and proceed up the tarmac road opposite the hotel drive. Reach the junction with the main road and turn right to **Kissonerga**. [This is where Geoff starts the walk, following the same route at first.] Turn left along the road which passes to right of the school, and pass the Old Folks' Home and adjoining cemetery on your left. At the T-junction turn left and, about 15min later, turn onto a track going diagonally left (with a row of tall conifers on the left). Arrive at a fenced area (at a junction of tracks), containing a water main and a valve wheel. Here the track swings right and follows the concrete watercourse on the right, which initially is covered with concrete slabs but from time to time is open. Follow this watercourse until until you reach tall gates blocking the way. Here turn left and walk downhill through orange groves. At the bottom the track swings to the left and continues down the valley in the opposite direction to the high watercourse route, but shortly climbs uphill where you turn right to the **Mavrokolymbos Dam**. Pass the dam wall and associated building on your right. Take the first left turn and climb uphill to the Coral Bay/Akoursos road. [Here the walk in the book goes *left*.] Here turn right and walk uphill on a tarmac

elephone No	Timetable
	enquire at the Paphos Tourist Office (not included in Cyprus Tourism timetables)
	enquire at the Paphos Tourist Office (not included in Cyprus Tourism timetables)
	enquire at the Paphos Tourist Office (not included in Cyprus Tourism timetables)
	enquire at the Paphos Tourist Office (not included in Cyprus Tourism timetables)

ɔad, then take first track off left, which t first runs diagonally to the road, then vings left to run down the valley. At T-junction of tracks (by an excava- on on your right), turn right. This ack then swings left and climbs eeply uphill, becoming very rough nderfoot. Continue ahead on this ack, walking generally parallel to the ea on your left. When the track drops eeply downhill and swings to the ght, bear left on a rather indistinct ath, cross the stream at the bottom of e hill and swing round to the left phill. Shortly, the path drops down- ill again to cross another stream and eet a track coming in from the right: rn left here. Shortly after passing a oat pen on your left, you arrive at a ossroads: turn left and head for the ea. Ignore all turns-offs but, when you ome to a large building (?: incom- ete at time of writing) on your left, ithin sight of the road spanning the alley, go diagonally right to join oral Bay/Peyia road at the end of the ash barrier. Turn left and walk down the Coral Bay road.' (User, 1/99)

/alk 12: The dirt road at the **start** is ow tarred, then concrete all the way Akoursos. (User, 3/99)

Valk 15: At the **25min**-point, just efore the valley floor, *turn right.* Jser, 3/99) • **Circular walk for motorists:** After passing the two gates at the **2h15min**-point, *ignore the first track on the left;* take the *second track to the left (200m/yds further on),* between a goat enclosure and a small farm. Continue gently uphill on the major track in more or less the same direction until you meet a goat farm, where the track goes left, then right, and reaches the ridge. Do *not* follow the track ahead here (through an orchard), but follow the stony path downhill to the right. (User, 4/00) • Another user (6/00) says the following: A new track leads out of the Khapotami gorge at a gentle gradient. You enter the gorge as before and simply follow the main track after the alternative path has joined in. The main track branches left from the original route at around the 1h25min-point and proceeds as a broad easy ascent levelling off after about 20 minutes. Some 15 minutes further on you reach the two gates at the vineyards. Walk through the two gates, taking care to close (and fasten) them behind you. Ignore a track that leads off at a sharp angle to the left after about 60 metres. For the circular route turn left at a rough road about 150 metres further on. This starts between fenced orchards and enters a "GAME RESERVE AREA". Follow this in a gentle ascent,

continues on page 128

Index

Geographical entries only are included in this index. For other entries see Contents, page 3. A page number in *italic type* indicates a map reference; a page number in **bold type** indicates a photograph or drawing. Both of these may be in addition to a text reference on the same page. *'TM'* refers to the large-scale walking map on the reverse of the touring map. Transport timetables are given on pages 113 to 125.

STOP PRESS (continued)

ignoring lesser tracks branching off. As you approach the hilltop through some trees, you come to a T-junction with a fenced off area ahead. Turn left and then after 75 metres or so, turn right, following the corner of the fenced off area. This leads over the top of the ridge. In clear weather you can see Pano Arkhimandrita across the valley towards the left. Follow the track which descends in zigzags to the streambed at Kato Arkimandrita.

Walk 16: The descent from Laoni Ridge is, as stated on page 81, not an absolute route. The scramble is quite straightforward however, although it may look a daunting prospect at first. Don't worry about getting lost... you can see the old road to Petra very clearly, and the manner of you arriving there need not be precise. (Author) • We found an easy way down the Laoni Ridge to the goat enclosure. We followed the track at the bottom but then came upon roadworks, which we followed first to the left and then to the right, before regaining the route in the book. (User, 3/99) • There may eventually be problems with the descent to Petra tou Romiou as the new motorway to Paphos is under construction and the route must cross it somewhere. (User, 6/00) • The farmhouse (**1h25min**; Picnic 16, photo page 16) has been renovated, but the threshing machine is still there. (User, 6/00)

Walk 18: I did this in the opposite direction. The advantage was that at the start of the walk I was fresher and could better appreciate the beautiful view over the deep blue sea. I climbed Pano Vakhines, and, although it was steep, it was easier going up than coming down a slippery path. (User, 10/99)... The descent was steep *and vertiginous; you must be sure-footed and have a head for heights.* (User, 6/00) • **Access:** There is a new Amorga bus from Paphos to Polis (Mon-Fri, from 09.00-14.00 hourly); there is a bus from Polis to the baths at 10.00, 12.00, 15.00. Returns from the Baths at 10.30, 12.30, 15.30; returns from Polis at 12.00, 13.45, 14.30, 16.0 17.00.

Walk 19: We forgot a torch, but *ther is a drop of about 2m/6ft inside th mine* (**1h30min**). (User, 6/00)

Walk 22: The road at the **start** of th walk is tarred until it clears the village The hillside of Ayios Yeoryios ma now be a military observation post an there is no access. (User, 3/99)

Walk 24: Apart from the summer-onl bus to Governors Beach, one can us the Nicosia (Kemek) or Larnac (Kallenos) service buses. They ru along the old road; alight at the turr off to Ayios Yeoryios. The buses the cross the motorway and go past th road junction where the walk end (where you show a 🚘 symbol on th map on page 89). (User)

Walk 25: What a drive to get there, bu it was worth it. The start is not eas now, as the road has been widened leaving a bank of 6 or 7ft to climb. W parked at the picnic site and walke from there. Where you leave the trac near the top, you now have to clim road barriers as well as scramble dow the bank. We had no problems gettin to the first cairn, but the second on was much more difficult. (User, 6/0

Walk 26: This walk is accessible by th Limassol/Nicosia bus (Timetable A4 which travels on the old road an passes the end of the Stavrovoun road.

Walk 27: After **40min** there is now a easy *inland* path well marked b cairns, for those who don't have walk ing boots... After **1h15min** the forestr department's 'nature trail' is now road. (User, 2/98)

Walk 28: Near the mast (**35min**) encountered watchful (not to sa paranoid) police. Walkers should b advised not to take photos here, look through binoculars for too lo (User, 1/98)